Wicked COLUMBIA

VICE AND VILLAINY IN THE CAPITAL

ALEXIA JONES HELSLEY

THE
History
PRESS

Published by The History Press
Charleston, SC 29403
www.historypress.net

First published 2013

Manufactured in the United States

ISBN 978.1.60949.850.4

Library of Congress CIP data applied for.

For Keiser and Justus
"Train up a child in the way he should go; and when he is old,
he will not depart from it."
Proverbs 22:6 (KJV)

Contents

Acknowledgements

T he author gratefully acknowledges the assistance of visual materials archivist Beth Bilderback, director Dr. Allen Stokes, Terry W. Lipscomb and Fritz Hamer of the South Caroliniana Library, University of South Carolina; archivist IV Marion Chandler, Brian Collars and director of reference services Steve Tuttle, the South Carolina Department of Archives and History; Debra Bloom, Walker Family and Local History Center manager, Richland County Library; director Jane Tuten and the staff of the Gregg-Graniteville Library, University of South Carolina–Aiken; and Janet Hudson. In addition, the author thanks photographers Jacob Helsley and Terry Helsley. As always, she owes a special debt to Terry Helsley for his indexing of this manuscript.

Prologue

Vice and villainy are as old as mankind. The first recorded murder appears in the book of Genesis, when Cain kills his brother Abel. Archaeologists have identified countless incidents of man's inhumanity to man. Ancient historians such as Procopius wrote of palace intrigues, poisonings, assassinations and prostitution. The essentials of untimely death, theft, fraud, abuse and victimization are enduring threads in the history of man's time on earth. New technologies alter the landscape of death and distrust, but, as Joseph Conrad wrote, from "the heart of darkness," there is no escape.

The midlands of South Carolina are no strangers to vice and villainy. The Spaniard Hernando deSoto and his men were the first known Europeans to enter the world of South Carolina's native peoples. His thirst for power and riches led him to abuse the hospitality of the lady of Cofitachequi. Such behavior set the tone for succeeding generations who made their homes near the confluence of the Broad and Saluda Rivers.

A young Englishman named James Lawson was probably the first Englishman to view the great forests and dangerous rapids of what would become South Carolina's capital city. He wrote of the flocks of passenger pigeons so thick that one could not see the sun and of immensely tall virgin forests. A visit to Congaree Swamp National Park offers a glimpse into that far away world.

But rivers are also natural conduits for trade and travel, and the native inhabitants had well-established trails that crisscrossed South Carolina.

After the English settlement at Charles Town in 1670, early settlers pushed their way into the interior seeking their fortunes. Some turned to commerce in the fledging city of Charles Town, others were planters seeking the perfect staple crop for economic success and still others pursued trade with native peoples, such as the Cherokee, Creek, Catawba, the ill-used Westo, the exploited Yemassee, the doomed Seewee and others. The major Indian trading path that connected Charles Town with these far-flung villages passed through the midlands. In fact, near the future site of Columbia, the trading path branched. One branch ran northwest to the Lower Cherokee towns of modern Pickens, Oconee and Greenville Counties. Another ran northward toward the Catawba Confederation, and the last ran westward to the Savannah River. To protect these trade routes, the colony established a series of fortifications, including Fort Moore on the Savannah and Fort Granby at the Congarees.

The early decades of settlement were turbulent ones for the Carolina interior. Lawson died during the Tuscarora War in North Carolina, and all of South Carolina's natives, except the Cherokee, rebelled and nearly destroyed the colony in 1715 during the Yemassee War. In time, peace and trade returned to the midlands, but new settlers brought new issues. In the 1730s, the new Royal governor Robert Johnson proposed a series of townships to facilitate the settlement of the interior. One of these townships, Saxe Gotha, lay near the Congarees. Many German-speaking Protestants settled there and in nearby Amelia.

George Haig was one of those who sought fame and fortune in the township of Saxe Gotha. Haig was a businessman, deputy surveyor and occasional government agent. He not only negotiated agreements for the colony with the Cherokee but also surveyed land allotments in the new township. He and his wife, Elizabeth, settled on Sandy Run, where he operated a trading post. At one point, Haig was in a Cherokee village on a mission for Colonial Governor James Glen. During his stay, he discovered that Iroquois braves had captured several South Carolina settlement Indians—natives who lived near colonial settlements. Angered by their enslavement, Haig demanded the immediate release of the captives. While Haig won the opening round, his victory was short-lived. In 1748 while on a trading expedition to the Catawba Nation, members of the Seneca tribe captured Haig, laughed when he begged on his knees for mercy and killed his horses. Not interested in ransom, his captors sent his indentured servant with a tomahawk to notify Haig's wife, Elizabeth, and then fled northward with their captive. Elizabeth Haig notified Governor Glen, who began diplomatic negotiations to rescue Haig, whom he termed "a most useful man." Nevertheless, rescue came too late. A year and a day after his capture, a Pennsylvania Indian agent found the village where Haig was being held. By that time, Haig, unfortunately, was dead. Despairing of rescue, he had taunted his captors until they killed him.

As a result of this frontier tragedy, colonial administrators reactivated Fort Granby and stationed an independent company there to defend the settlers. In time, Lieutenant Peter Mercier, a member of this company, married the widow Haig. Shortly thereafter, Mercier volunteered for service against the French and died heroically at the Battle of Great Meadows in Pennsylvania, a triggering event for the French and Indian War. For her third matrimonial attempt, Elizabeth Haig Mercier married a retired veteran, David Webb, who survived her. Life on the South Carolina frontier was demanding and outcomes often unexpected.

FRONTIER HERESY

One of the more exciting and definitely unexpected chapters of the early history of the Midlands was the so-called Weberite heresy. In an area with few churches and fewer ministers, laymen often attempted to fill the void with house prayer meetings and Bible study. Jacob Weber was one of these involved laymen. In this instance, unfortunately, Weber saw his calling differently. He envisioned himself as God the Father, and his wife, Hannah, as the Virgin Mary. He designated a neighbor named Peter Schmidt, or Schmidtpeter, as Jesus Christ and an African American as the Holy Spirit.

Perhaps little would be known of this frontier religious expression, except that Weber condemned the so-called Holy Spirit as Satan and led his followers in killing him. By some accounts, the congregants piled on the unfortunate man and crushed him to death. When word of the backcountry sect reached Charlestown, authorities there arrested Weber, Jacob Geiger, another adherent, and the other known leaders. On February 24, 1761, Weber and others were tried in Charlestown, found guilty and hanged. The courts convicted the others as well but pardoned Weber's wife.

VIGILANTE VIOLENCE

As Charlestown, the capital, was the center of law enforcement for the colony, Midlands residents lacked local access to justice. The only courts in the colony were in Charlestown. As a result, they were unprepared to cope with the violence of the postwar period. Following the French and Indian War, armed racially mixed bands terrorized the law-abiding inhabitants. With justice so far removed, the locals had little redress. To exacerbate the situation, when a handful of miscreants were detained and sent to the capital for trial, the newly arrived royal governor Charles Montagu pardoned them as a gesture of good will.

At that point, some residents, styling themselves "regulators," joined forces to attack the problem. These regulators brought vigilante justice to the area, and in 1769 Colonial authorities created a system of circuit courts for the backcountry. Yet conflict returned during the American Revolution, as Patriots and Loyalists vied for the loyalty of these frontiersmen. A major British supply route crossed the area (the old Cherokee path) and partisans raided British shipments while competing Loyalist and Patriot militia made life dangerous on the home front.

Chapter 1
Birth of a City

After years of civil bloodshed, the Revolutionary War at last ended. British troops and thousands of Loyalists finally left Charlestown on December 14, 1782. The Treaty of Paris was officially signed September 3, 1783. But the cessation of war did not end the conflict. Loyalists attempted to reclaim their lives, and Patriots with long memories vowed vengeance. The disaffected and alienated formed racially mixed gangs and preyed on poorly defended remote farms and unwary travelers. When the South Carolina legislature reconvened in 1782, the representatives confiscated Loyalist property to punish them for their allegiance to the king. But bigger issues threatened the new state.

Since the 1730s, population in the backcountry as it was known had grown, and by the 1780s, the majority of South Carolinians lived above the fall zone—the former seacoast that runs through parts of Aiken, Lexington, Richland, Kershaw and Sumter Counties. The sand hills from that ancient shoreline now stretch across central South Carolina. During the Revolution, these upstate or backcountry men were instrumental in key Patriot victories—for example, at King's Mountain and Cowpens. Consequently, after the fighting ended and peace came, they wanted equal representation in the new state legislature, property taxation based on the value of the land and other accommodations. In other words, they wanted political equality.

One of the results of this power struggle was a debate over the location of a new capital. Backcountry representatives demanded a more accessible central location. Thomas Sumter pushed Stateburg as a viable alternative,

The Congarees. The South Carolina General Assembly placed the new capital of Columbia near the confluence of the Broad and Saluda Rivers. The rivers flow together to form the Congaree River. *State Historic Preservation Office, Lexington County. Courtesy of the South Carolina Department of Archives and History.*

but the legislative instead selected the Plains, the Taylor Plantation just below the convergence of the Broad and Saluda Rivers.

So, in 1786 South Carolina had a new capital—a planned city laid out on a grid with broad streets, 100–150 feet wide—situated in the center of the state. The new town, according to Robert Mills, was two miles square and stood on a high plain on the east bank of the Congaree River. On September 26, 1786, the commissioners offered the first lots for sale. The advertisement touted level land and a healthy situation, lying between the juncture of the Broad and Saluda Rivers and Friday's Ferry. The site of the new town also boasted two miles of frontage on the Congaree River.

Yet, while upcountry residents were excited about an accessible capital, many Lowcountry residents resented the move and in 1790 staged a last-ditch effort to return the capital to Charleston. Representatives and senators clashed in the statehouse, gentlemen fought duels and street fights were common.

Nevertheless, the new town grew slowly as legislators only stayed in Columbia during the legislative session—a few months at best. So when George Washington visited Columbia in May 1791, he described the town as "an uncleared wood, with very few houses in it, and those all wooden over." He found the wooden statehouse "commodious" but unfinished. Other visitors noted that the houses were usually "painted gray and yellow." The streets were unpaved, and by 1808, at least a third of the city's streets were still not open, but trees lined Columbia's Richardson (Main) Street.

Despite its limited beginnings and small population, in time, the new capital prospered. On December 18, 1799, the South Carolina General Assembly made Columbia the courthouse town for Richland District (County). The new county seat offered additional services and attracted a permanent population. In 1816, the town had perhaps 250 dwellings and almost one thousand residents. In 1831, Anne Royall found Columbia "flourishing" and "handsome." In 1840, the city's population exceeded four thousand. By 1856, James Wood Davidson wrote to a friend, "Columbia was out in its spring attire of roses and floral gems. Oh! It is a lovely and loveable place."

Yet Columbia was not an oasis of morality in the midlands. Pickpockets, confidence men and ladies of the evening walked the unpaved streets and plied their trades in the drab hotels and boardinghouses. Gamblers and confidence men found victims among the visitors and incomers. Forgers added their special touch to this volatile mix.

The pickpockets were so blatant that not even Columbia's mayor escaped. At one point, Chief of Police Josh Snowden informed Captain Henry Lyons, mayor, of a dispatch from Augusta alerting Columbia that a well-known pickpocket was en route to Columbia. In 1850, Lyons, the intendant, or mayor, of Columbia, owned real estate valued at $18,500. Later, the mayor and one of his aldermen, Colonel Maybin (possibly William Maybin who operated a hotel in Columbia in 1850), took a walk along Bull Street. There, they encountered a respectably attired man. The stranger, seemingly impressed with his surroundings, lauded the beauty of Columbia. Quite excited by the interest, the mayor and stranger talked some time and then parted. Much later, the mayor was surprised to discover his wallet missing. A few days later, a passerby found the mayor's empty wallet in the Presbyterian churchyard near where the mayor walked earlier—a souvenir for the mayor of his encounter with the charming pickpocket.

First Presbyterian Church. Mayor Lyons found his empty wallet in the churchyard. *Photograph by Jacob H. Helsley.*

According to Jack Kenny Williams, Columbia was "a gathering place for fakirs [*sic*], swindlers and idlers." Newcomers even complained that, unlike neighboring Lexington, Columbia residents needed to lock their doors and windows. In 1855, the *Daily South Carolinian* noted that Columbia's miscreants, not satisfied with merely robbing city visitors, had begun burglarizing homes and businesses.

Chapter 2

Coming of Age

As the county seat, Columbia had a jail and courthouse. Perhaps bowing to necessity, the jail was the first building constructed. The contract specified a two-story brick building. By 1805, the courthouse was also operational. Joel McLemore was Richland County's first sheriff. Columbia was also a municipal center, and the first city hall was open for business by 1818.

Columbia's first market began on the ground floor of the city hall, which stood on Main (then Richardson) Street. Vendors offered fresh meat, vegetables and other products. By 1860, vendors began moving to Assembly Street. There was more space there for vendors. In addition to South Carolina agricultural products, the Columbia market was also an outlet for crops and livestock from Western North Carolina and eastern Tennessee. In addition to buyers and sellers, the market attracted pickpockets, confidence men and prostitutes. The city's red-light district grew up nearby. Columbia resident E.F. Williams wrote of a killing at the market. From Williams's account, a Confederate soldier angered over the eviction of his wife and children took matters into his own hands. Deserting, he traveled to Columbia, surprised the landlord at the market and killed him.

The market was possibly a factor in a December 1820 death. On the evening of December 28, a North Carolina wagoner and his son were passing through Columbia. Near the town limits, they encountered a man on horseback. A verbal argument ensued, and as the man rode off, the son heard a rock or brick pass the wagon. Another rock or brick then struck the wagoner above the temple. The man, although stunned, tried to continue while his assailant disappeared down a side street. About two miles outside of Columbia, the man collapsed. Carried to a nearby dwelling, the man lingered through the night and died the following morning. An examination revealed a fractured cranium—the likely cause of death. According to the newspaper, the supposed "perpetrator of this horrid deed" was arrested that evening.

In 1808, Columbia's first police force had one marshal but with limited responsibilities. Such a minimal presence did little to deter crime, but by 1824, Columbia had a police force of ten with twenty-four-hour responsibilities. Still, with a population of six thousand, the ten policemen with their rotating schedules faced an uphill struggle to maintain law and order. In 1855, residents complained that thieves daily robbed homes with impunity. Echoing a familiar refrain, one even asked, "What are our city authorities about?"

PUNISHMENT

When miscreants were apprehended and convicted, Columbia and other antebellum towns offered an array of punishments. Many involved public spectacles such as branding, whipping and hanging. In South Carolina, the sheriff branded convicted criminals usually with the letters "M," "F" and "T," depending on the crime. The letter "M" was used for those convicted of murder or manslaughter, "T" for theft and "F" for felon. Not all those convicted were branded. In the pre-revolutionary world, this medieval relic normally accompanied an appeal to benefit of clergy. While other punishments, such as the pillory, ended with the revolution, branding persisted into the early nineteenth century, but it was used rarely, and by mid-century, fines replaced branding for those convicted of manslaughter.

County seats such as Columbia had public whipping posts. Whipping was the usual penalty for property crimes. Public whippings occurred frequently and were deemed a particularly demeaning punishment— especially for a white man. Given the punishment's association with slave discipline, white men and women who were whipped often disappeared after their punishment. Sheriffs or jailers administered the blows. During sentencing, the judge set the number of lashes and the timetable for administration. Yet public revulsion let to legislative efforts to limit and eventually abolish the practice. So by the 1850s, public whippings, at least of white men, were rare. J.F. Williams, who moved to Columbia in 1856, remembered two jewel thieves who were sentenced to jail time—twelve months—and a monthly whipping of thirty-nine lashes each. According to Williams, after the first whipping, the two men escaped from jail and fled the area. By the time the state seceded, other forms of punishment— particularly incarceration and fines—replaced whipping.

Until 1868, law enforcement executed felons by hanging, usually at Potter's Field in Columbia. Julian Selby, who recorded his memories in *Memorabilia and Anecdotal Reminiscences of Columbia, South Carolina*, published in 1905 and also published the *Columbia Phoenix* (1865–78), remembered a rare triple hanging. Shortly after he moved to Columbia as a young child in the 1830s, slaves from the boardinghouse where he lived with his mother took him to see the unusual hanging of three slaves. The men who were hanged had been convicted of killing McCaskill, an overseer for the Singletons. The Singletons owned a plantation, Kensington, in the Eastover area. Not all executions occurred on schedule. For example, on June 3, 1838, the *Charleston Courier* reported a temporary reprieve. Governor Pierce M. Butler of South Carolina temporarily reprieved John Adams until July 1838. Adams, convicted of the murder of Mrs. M'Voy, was originally sentenced to be hanged on May 30. J.F. Williams recalled that "his first impression" of Columbia in 1856 was a gallows. Apparently, shortly before Williams moved to Columbia, officials hanged a man named McCombs for killing a policeman named Cross, perhaps David H. Cross. From 1868 until 1912, criminals were hanged in the county jail or jail yard. After 1912, the state penitentiary in Columbia was the site for all legal executions. The electric chair was installed that same year.

THE JAIL

Having a jail was essential to good order, but keeping the jail in order was difficult. Throughout the antebellum years, residents were often concerned about the condition of the jail. In 1806 the Richland District Grand Jury expressed concern that the jail was not "kept in better order" and that "the insufficiency of the Goal" was a factor in a recent jailbreak. Matters

Washington Street looking east, by Walter L. Blanchard, 1913. *Courtesy of South Caroliniana Library, University of South Carolina (Photographs 8351-11).*

did not improve, and in 1827, the grand jury again complained that the jail was "insufficient for the purposes for which it was intended." The jury contended that the facility was not only an insecure place to house prisoners, but also "too small to give safe and proper accommodation" for the prisoners detained there. In particular, the jail only had four rooms. Two housed criminals, one was used for debtors and the fourth held runaway slaves. Consequently, there was no space for women, and the slave space was often "crowded by both sexes." According to the jury, the commingling of men and women in the jail was "such an exposure to temptation and vice" that immediate action was needed to remedy the situation.

By 1836, the county had improved the condition of the jail. Nevertheless, the grand jury's inspection still revealed poor maintenance by the jailer. Specially, the jury commented on missing pavement as well as broken windows in the kitchen. In 1838, the jury also recommended improved ventilation for the slave quarters. The county had a jail, but the city maintained a guardhouse.

The report of Mayor Allen J. Green provides a window into guardhouse operation. According to his report, between March 1859 and March 1860, the guardhouse on Washington Street housed 650 slaves, 234 white prisoners and 40 free blacks. Most of the slaves were incarcerated for being out past curfew or difficulties with their owners. The majority of white and free black prisoners were generally locked up for drunkenness and disorderly conduct. These statistics suggest that Columbia's police were not idle.

Affairs of Honor

A morbid fascination surrounds South Carolina's devotion to the *code duello*—the code of honor. Elite South Carolinians jeopardized their lives and those of friends, colleagues and other social equals to defend their honor. According to Jack Kenny Williams, duels were popular in South Carolina and other Southern states before 1825 and still a major avenue of conflict resolution for elite southerners between then and the Civil War. While some appealed to chivalry as a root cause for dueling in the South, others, such as historian Clement Eaton, contended that dueling reflected the military mindset of antebellum southerners. Personal justice appealed to a frontier mentality and, perhaps, a culture of machismo.

Dueling, like gambling, managed to persist despite legislative prohibitions. For example, in 1823, the state of South Carolina passed "An Act to explain and amend an act, entitled 'an act to prevent the pernicious practice of Duelling.'" This act provided that anyone involved with a duel could be "compelled to give evidence…without criminating himself." Throughout the antebellum years, the legislature tried to find a legal remedy to gentlemen's affairs of honor.

The code of honor appealed especially to South Carolina elite, who favored such an extra-legal method of problem solving. According to the *City Gazette* of Charleston, rumors circulated in January 1791 that General Isaac Huger (1748–1797) and Colonel Wade Hampton (1752–1835) had fought a duel in Columbia. Both men were Revolutionary War veterans. At the time, no additional details were provided.

In 1802, the Richland District Grand Jury protested "against the unlawful, the odious, the disgusting, and distressing practice of Duelling." In 1804, the grand jurors again complained "against the unlawful, the odious, the depopulating, and disgusting practice of Duelling." Despite frequent presentments from the Richland District Grand Jury, gentlemen continued to pursue their "affairs of honor." In 1803, the South Carolina Society of the Cincinnati and the American Revolution Society sent a memorial to the state legislature asking legal measures to "restrain the practice of dueling." In the petition, society members argued dueling was a "pernicious custom"; that "this moral vengeance is not resorted to merely in cases of grievous injuries…but in many cases of trivial offence;" that dueling "decides no right, and settles no point as….the innocent and aggrieved person is as likely to be the victim, as the guilty offender"; and that the custom was "in direct hostility to the principles of Christianity."

According to Edwin Scott, in the early 1820s, Chapman Levy, who had moved to Columbia from Camden, faced Dr. James H. Taylor, son of Governor John Taylor (1770–1832), in a duel. John Taylor served as the governor of South Carolina from 1826 to 1828. Taylor's brother William Taylor killed Dr. Cheeseborough, a young doctor, allegedly for "improper intimacy" with Taylor's wife. The killing happened at William Taylor's home in Lexington. The prosecution asked Levy to assist. William Taylor was tried for murder but acquitted. This is not the first time an alleged adulterer paid the ultimate price for his or her indiscretion, and a South Carolina jury acquitted the murderer.

Despite the successful (from the Taylors' perspective) outcome, Levy's comments during the proceedings offended Dr. James H. Taylor. Later, when Levy and James Taylor met in Columbia, Taylor struck Levy, and as a consequence, a duel ensued. On January 12, 1821, the two men met on the field of honor. Levy's shot missed Taylor, but Taylor wounded Levy below his right knee. Levy recovered.

In 1833, William Campbell Preston, a native of Pennsylvania, and Robert Cunningham arranged a duel. According to Preston, who lived in Columbia, Cunningham of Hamburg had made a "wanton attack" on him "through the public press," and as a result, he had "no alternative, but to demand the satisfaction usual amongst gentlemen." Cunningham accepted the challenge, but at the last minute, their seconds settled the matter. Apparently, Preston, a member of the South Carolina General Assembly until his election in 1833 to the United States Senate, had denounced the conduct of South Carolina Loyalists during the American Revolution. Unfortunately, Cunningham, whose family included Loyalists, had taken umbrage. Once Cunningham understood that Preston's remarks were not personal, the affair ended amicably. William Campbell Preston (1794–1860) was also an attorney and United States Senator (1833–1842). Preston, a graduate of South Carolina College, was one of antebellum South Carolina's great orators and is buried at Trinity Episcopal Cathedral in Columbia.

Senator William Campbell Preston. In 1833, Preston and Robert Cunningham arranged a duel. *Copy of a portrait (Photographs 2543), Courtesy of South Caroliniana Library, University of South Carolina.*

While the cause of Robert Cunningham's "attack" on Preston is not known, several individuals named Cunningham loyally supported the king during the American Revolution. One of them, William "Bloody Bill" Cunningham was an infamous Tory who terrorized much of Old Ninety Six District—especially his home county of Laurens and neighboring counties of Newberry and Edgefield. William Cunningham earned his name by wanton attacks and his "take no prisoners" policy. A vengeful man, he spared neither young nor old but managed to die peacefully in his bed.

Politics were also a factor in a controversy involving A.S. Johnson and A.H. Pemberton. The election of 1840 was a particularly exciting one in Columbia. The Whigs organized early in support of their candidates—William Henry Harrison and John Tyler. Johnson and Pemberton were newspaper editors on a collision course. Johnson supported the Whigs, and Pemberton edited the Democratic paper. The Whigs carried Richland District, but the Columbia-area voters elected Democratic candidates. So the Democratic-controlled legislature awarded state printing contracts to Pemberton. This decision outraged Johnson, who had formerly had the state contract. When the two men met in Columbia, Johnson struck Pemberton in Main Street. Nevertheless, rather than demand satisfaction, Pemberton, according to Scott, "let the insult pass."

Even members of the South Carolina legislature were not immune to "affairs of honor." Again, given the time frame, politics could have been involved. Joseph A. Black, Justice of the Quorum for Richland District, contacted the South Carolina Senate with dangerous news. On oath, R.W. Barnwell, president of South Carolina College, had deposed that Daniel E. Huger and A.M. Rhett planned to "break the peace by sending & accepting a challenge to fight and by fighting a duel." In consequence of this information, Black required Huger to give his "recognizance to keep the peace" or else be prosecuted for breaking the law. Daniel E. Huger (1799–1854) owned Goodwill Plantation in Richland District and served in the South Carolina House of Representatives and Senate. A Federalist and Unionist during the Nullification controversy, Huger was also a member of the United States Senate. In 1850, Black was a forty-eight-year-old attorney living in Columbia.

The spark for the alleged duel occurred in the South Carolina Senate, so the date for the altercation falls between 1838 and 1841, the years of Huger's two terms in the South Carolina Senate. Black also sent a copy of Barnwell's written statement to the South Carolina Senate's Committee on Privileges and Elections. Nevertheless, as Black noted, Barnwell's information did not include specifics of the altercation between Huger and Rhett. However, he declared that the information he received convinced him that a duel was intended, and he issued a warrant. Barnwell had told Black that "the personal & intimate friend of one of the gentlemen concerned had come to Columbia the morning after the altercation in the senate." Black's letter to the senate committee has an apologetic tone. But in his defense, Black wrote that if "these gentlemen had fought and either of them unhappily had lost his life and society a valuable member," he could not have forgiven himself.

An Abbeville newspaper reported in 1854 that Richland District sheriff Charles Neuffer had interrupted a duel at the racecourse, a few miles from Columbia. Neuffer, a native of Germany, appears on the 1850 census as a deputy sheriff. Reportedly, two South Carolina College students had planned a duel for 5:00 p.m. The students, their seconds and friends arrived and one participant had loaded their pistols before the sheriff surprised them. Nevertheless, after the young men promised not to duel in Richland District, the sheriff released them. The combatants planned a venue change to North Carolina, but fortunately, friends intervened and successfully adjudicated the differences.

In 1851, although not necessarily an affair of honor, two leading Columbians exchanged blows on Main (Richardson). On April 15, 1851, Jesse E. Dent and Robert P. Mayrant encountered each other, and an argument ensued. Mayrant stabbed Dent with a pocketknife. In retaliation, Dent, later a Richland County sheriff, hit Mayrant on the head with a hammer. In 1850, the census listed Dent as a forty-year-old man. Robert P. Mayrant, according to the 1850 census, was a planter with real estate valued at $24,000. According to historian John Hammond Moore, no other details of this incident are available, but both men survived.

Later in 1857, two unidentified men were in Columbia making arrangements for a meeting of honor. Unfortunately for their purposes, Sheriff Jesse Dent learned of the matter and intervened. As a result, both men were bound to keep the peace, and the duel did not occur—at least not in Richland County.

As a postscript, in 1975, workmen at the University of South Carolina cut down a historic oak tree. According to an account in the *Columbia Record*, federal soldiers had tied their horses to the tree during the federal occupation

Jonathan Maxcy Monument. Maxcy was the first president of South Carolina College. *Photograph by Terry L. Helsley.*

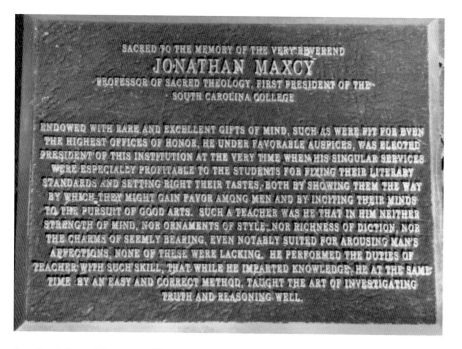

SACRED TO THE MEMORY OF THE VERY REVEREND
JONATHAN MAXCY
PROFESSOR OF SACRED THEOLOGY, FIRST PRESIDENT OF THE
SOUTH CAROLINA COLLEGE

ENDOWED WITH RARE AND EXCELLENT GIFTS OF MIND, SUCH AS WERE FIT FOR EVEN
THE HIGHEST OFFICES OF HONOR, HE UNDER FAVORABLE AUSPICES, WAS ELECTED
PRESIDENT OF THIS INSTITUTION AT THE VERY TIME WHEN HIS SINGULAR SERVICES
WERE ESPECIALLY PROFITABLE TO THE STUDENTS FOR FIXING THEIR LITERARY
STANDARDS AND SETTING RIGHT THEIR TASTES, BOTH BY SHOWING THEM THE WAY
BY WHICH THEY MIGHT GAIN FAVOR AMONG MEN AND BY INCITING THEIR MINDS
TO THE PURSUIT OF GOOD ARTS. SUCH A TEACHER WAS HE THAT IN HIM NEITHER
STRENGTH OF MIND, NOR ORNAMENTS OF STYLE, NOR RICHNESS OF DICTION, NOR
THE CHARMS OF SEEMLY BEARING, EVEN NOTABLY SUITED FOR AROUSING MAN'S
AFFECTIONS, NONE OF THESE WERE LACKING. HE PERFORMED THE DUTIES OF
TEACHER WITH SUCH SKILL, THAT WHILE HE IMPARTED KNOWLEDGE, HE AT THE SAME
TIME BY AN EASY AND CORRECT METHOD, TAUGHT THE ART OF INVESTIGATING
TRUTH AND REASONING WELL.

Jonathan Maxcy Monument, University of South Carolina Horseshoe, Sumter Street. *Photograph by Terry L. Helsley.*

and two students, with professors serving as seconds, had dueled under the hanging limbs. On January 15, 1975, the tree was removed. Why? Some feared a falling branch would damage the Maxcy monument.

Noted South Carolina architect Robert Mills designed the Maxcy monument, an obelisk similar in design to the Washington Monument, also designed by Mills. In addition, among his many accomplishments, Mills designed the Fireproof Building in Charleston, numerous South Carolina courthouses and the United States Treasury Building in Washington, D.C. In 1827, the monument, which honors Jonathan Maxcy, the first president of South Carolina College, was erected in the center of the University of South Carolina's historic Horseshoe. On April 28, 1804, the trustees elected Maxcy as the college's first president. The brilliant and highly respected Maxcy was a Baptist and a Federalist from Rhode Island who had previously served as president of Brown University in Providence, Rhode Island, and Union College in Schenectady, New York. The USC Bucket List, a website, lists climbing the Maxcy Monument as number 77 on a list of "100 things all Gamecocks should do before they graduate."

SOUTH CAROLINA COLLEGE

As part of the effort to reconcile backcountry and Lowcountry differences, in 1801, the South Carolina General Assembly chartered the South Carolina College. The plan worked well for the state's future. In the decades leading to the Civil War, many South Carolina College graduates served in the legislature and as governors. But in the meantime, the students of South Carolina College were a particular challenge for college administrators, city governance and law enforcement. South Carolina College rules prohibited drunkenness, dueling, forgery, card playing, swearing, cross-dressing, sexual relations, frequenting taverns, playing musical instruments during study periods and having firearms or liquor on campus. Such restrictions made discipline—or the lack thereof—a continuing problem for campus and city authorities. There were petty thefts, street scuffles and widespread drunkenness.

In fact, dealing with the often excitable young men was not only challenging but also dangerous at times. In 1846, a group of armed students encountered a policeman named Beaufill (perhaps Peter Bofil) on the third floor of a campus building. The students wanted to throw him over the railing—to his death or severe disability. Fortunately, a voice of reason—Giles Peterson, another student—intervened, and the students

Historic Horseshoe, University of South Carolina. Central News Company, Columbia, South Carolina. *Collection of the author.*

only pushed Beaufill down the stairs. Students not only antagonized the local constabulary but also threatened professors, gambled on campus and passed out drunk on the Horseshoe. In 1810, according to Daniel Hollis, students broke a window in the president's house and damaged residential property in Columbia. The rules of the college required that students who sent or received a challenge to duel—even if not actual duel participants—were liable for expulsion.

STUDENT DUELS

The prewar years saw several major college disturbances, including duels, campus disturbances and riots. In 1828, two students disagreed, and a challenge was issued and accepted. The students involved were James D. Tradewell and Jonathan Waters. Waters challenged Tradewell, but cooler-headed friends mediated the difficulty, and the duel was averted.

In May 1833, regrettably, there was no mediation. The tragic "dish of trout" duel involved two students, James G. Adams, son of Dr. William Adams, of Richland District, and A. Govan Roach of Colleton (Charleston) District. Roach and Adams were friends and customarily ate together. Unfortunately, one evening, they clashed during a meal at steward's hall (the college's boarding facility). Upon entering the dining hall, both reached for a platter of trout at the same time. Apparently, it was the custom that whoever first touched a dish had the right to reserve it for his personal use, so students competed to see who could reach the table first. The two friends glared at each other, and initially neither would relinquish the dish. Roach eventually released the dish but warned Adams that he would see him after dinner.

Regrettably, the conflict escalated into a duel of honor. In October 1833, the principals met with pistols at Lightwood Knot Springs (or Rice Creek Springs, per an article in the *Charleston Courier*), six miles north of Columbia and site of a military encampment during the Civil War. Both Adams and Roach were seriously wounded. Roach shot Adams in the abdomen, and in return, Adams shot Roach through the upper thigh and broke the bone. Adams died within a few hours of the duel. On October 19, 1833, the Euphradian Literary Society voted to drape its rostrum with crape in memory of Adams. South Carolina College trustees suspended and later expelled Robert W. Campbell from Marlboro County and George

Hailes from Richland County, who had served as seconds for Adams and Roach. Roach, lamed by his wound, returned home. Although he lived several more years, he never recovered physically or mentally from the deadly encounter.

Student Unrest

In addition to the Adams-Roach duel, student unrest aggravated relations between faculty and students and between town and gown. Students played pranks, destroyed property, pilfered and boisterously pursued the vices available in the capital city. The first altercation that affected almost the entire student body occurred in 1814. At that time, student unrest focused on Professor George Blackburn, who taught mathematics. Blackburn, a native of Ireland, was a gifted mathematician and astronomer trained at Trinity College in Dublin. In 1800, he moved his family to Philadelphia and later opened a school in Virginia. From 1804 to 1811, Blackburn taught mathematics at the College of William and Mary. In 1811, he became professor of Mathematics and Astronomy at South Carolina College. To Blackburn, the students were poorly prepared for college studies and had no interest in their education. In addition, the sometimes-cantankerous Blackburn was a stern disciplinarian who ridiculed his students and regularly reported students for infractions. Consequently, students did not appreciate Blackburn's attitude or his actions.

The simmering unrest came to a boil in February 1814. Blackburn and a tutor encountered three students trying to steal the college bell. He reported their actions, and the trustees expelled the students. Two of the students threatened Blackburn, and on February 8, the students, in disguise, burned an effigy of Blackburn, damaged the library and destroyed the bell. The students then marched en masse and attacked the rooms of the tutor and the home of Blackburn. College administrators could not restore order, and the Columbia militia had to intervene. As a result of this unrest, rather than continue at South Carolina College, Blackburn resigned. He left Columbia and moved to Baltimore, where he taught at the College of Asbury. In 1823, after his return to the capital city, Blackburn died in Columbia. As a sidelight on this talented man, in 1813, Blackburn accompanied an expedition to determine the western boundary between North and South Carolina. There, he saw Table Rock and wrote the following lines:

From the rock called the Table plantations are seen
That look as dark spots on a carpet of green

Blackburn also petitioned the South Carolina legislature for permission to "produce an accurate map of the State."

In addition to conflicts on campus, relations between town and gown were strained. Clashes between the law and the students persisted. For example, the police jailed a brother of Preston Brooks. Armed with a pistol, Brooks immediately rushed the jail and threatened to shoot the police. As a consequence, the trustees expelled Brooks, and he never received his degree.

PRESTON S. BROOKS.
REPRESENTATIVE IN CONGRESS OF THE U.S. FROM SOUTH CAROLINA.
EQUAL RIGHTS TO THE SOUTH AS WELL AS TO THE NORTH.
PUBLISHED BY C. BOHN, WASHINGTON D.C.

Preston Brooks was a United States Congressman from Edgefield District, South Carolina. As a South Carolina College student, he attacked the Columbia guardhouse to free his brother. *Engraved by Adam B. Walter, LC-USZC4-12608, Courtesy of the Library of Congress.*

Later, during the heated debates over slavery in the territories, as a United States Congressman, Preston Brooks gained national attention. On May 22, 1856, Brooks and fellow South Carolina congressman Lawrence Keitt entered the United States Senate Chamber. Brooks then attacked Massachusetts senator Charles Sumner as he sat at his desk. Brooks caned Sumner until the unconscious man slumped to the floor. Sumner was gripping his desk so tightly that he ripped it loose from the bolts holding it to the floor. Sumner regained consciousness but took years to recover. Eventually, he returned to his seat in the United States Senate.

Brooks alleged that Sumner, in a speech entitled, "The Crime Against Kansas," had defamed the honor of his uncle, Senator Andrew P. Butler. In the course of the address, Sumner referred to, among other things, Butler's unfortunate practice of spitting when he spoke and ridiculed Butler's proslavery stance, charging that he had taken "a mistress… who, though ugly to others, is always lovely to him…the harlot, Slavery." Deeming Sumner, as a Yankee, unworthy of a challenge, Sumner instead attacked him with a cane—similar to one used to discipline dogs. The caning of Sumner made headlines nationally. In the North, newspapers hailed Sumner as a martyr to the cause of abolition, while the Southern states fêted Brooks as a hero. Southern communities held banquets, and admirers mailed him new canes or wrote asking for pieces of the cane that hit Sumner. Brooks resigned from Congress, but South Carolina voters reelected him. Unfortunately for him, he died in 1857 before he could return to Washington.

Food Fight

In addition to the Brooks incident, there were other conflicts. Some of these involved discipline, conflict with law enforcement or the perennial food "fight." In 1852, one hundred students demanded an end to the practice of compulsory meal attendance.

In 1806, South Carolina College, in an effort to solve the problem of how to feed the students, erected a steward's hall (commons). The establishment of a communal dining hall triggered a long and often acrimonious reaction. The rationale was good. The college wanted to provide inexpensive meals for the students, save them time and reduce their exposure to temptation.

Students resented the compulsory nature of the arrangement and often found reasons to complain of the quality of the food (sounds familiar to any undergraduate). The position of steward was a challenging and thankless one and, at times, a difficult one to fill. Annual protests were de rigueur, as President Maxcy admitted. The students also annually filed petitions to have the compulsory commons system abolished. In 1827, under President Thomas Cooper, eighty students resolved to quit the commons and board in town. Cooper refused, and the students boycotted the commons. Cooper and the faculty demanded that the students return to the commons or be expelled. As a result, seventy-five students left. Some returned, and the trustees expelled the rest, including seniors. Thus Cooper successfully faced down the first student food revolt.

Yet the students also had cause for celebration. In 1828, the trustees ended compulsory commons and voted to permit the students to dine at certain approved establishments. However, in 1835, they reinstituted the compulsory system, hired a bursar and reinstated the requirement that students eat together on campus. While the new arrangement was preferable to the old steward's hall, problems persisted.

In 1852, during President James Henry Thornwell's first year in office, the students staged a major uprising known as the "Great Biscuit Rebellion." This revolt involved most of the enrolled student body. That fall, 108 students demanded that the trustees abolish the compulsory commons and reinstate access to off-campus approved boarding facilities. If the trustees did not act promptly, the students threatened to withdraw from school. The trustees refused, and the students withdrew. Ironically, given the interrupted studies and student angst, the next year the trustees approved a voluntary arrangement and also allowed the students to eat at certain licensed boardinghouses. Dr. Thornwell (1812–1862), a well-respected Presbyterian minister, went on to earn the students' affection and support. He resigned the college presidency in 1855 to become a professor of theology at the Presbyterian Seminary in Columbia.

GUARDHOUSE FRACAS

In 1856, South Carolina College had a new president, Charles F. McCay, who suffered by comparison with his eminent predecessor, Dr. James H. Thornwell. McCay, before his promotion, was a recently hired professor of mathematics and mechanical philosophy. Before coming to South Carolina College, McCay was professor of mathematics at the University of Georgia from 1833 to 1835 and, later, an insurance pioneer.

Nevertheless, on the evening of February 17, 1856, a long-standing feud between Columbia police and the students came to a head. In a classic town/gown conflict, a drunken student named Edward Niles had words with John Burdell, town marshal or chief of police. According to the 1860 census, Chief Burdell lived at Powell's Boarding House and at that time, owned real estate valued at $7,000. The police had a two-story brick guardhouse on

Main Campus, University of South Carolina (Horseshoe). *Courtesy of South Caroliniana Library, University of South Carolina (Postcards rich co 410).*

Main Street. The adjacent jail faced Washington Street. Regrettably, both facilities burned during the Civil War.

The confrontation escalated, and the combatants came to blows. As a result, Burdell's officers, including James Rose who lived on Washington Street, dragged Niles to the guardhouse. The student's friends quickly spread word of the incident, and a large number of students gathered at the guardhouse. Two of them attacked Burdell, and the situation was tense. President McCay attempted unsuccessfully to calm the students and restore order. E.J. Arthur, mayor of Columbia, called out the militia, and the students returned to campus. On campus, they raided the cadet arsenal stored in the library and armed themselves. Burdell released Niles, and McCay and the mayor decided to let a panel of citizens review the situation, make a recommendation and, if necessary, dismiss Burdell and the other officers.

The students, surprisingly, refused to agree to the proposal. Some of them did not think Burdell had suffered enough and hurried to the guardhouse. At that juncture, the overwhelmed McCay rallied the college professors. Bystanders were treated to the spectacle of armed students racing toward the guardhouse, pursued by the president and faculty. The mayor ordered the bell rung—a signal of alarm—and Sheriff Jesse E. Dent asked the

Civil War–era Columbia police force. During the antebellum years, South Carolina students and Columbia police had numerous clashes. John Burdell was the police chief in 1860. Resident E.F. Williams identified members of the police force as William Baugh, Paul Bofil, J.M. Coker, Michael Grimstead, Thomas Harrison, James W. Rose, Jackson Starling, James W. Sill and W.C. Strickland. *From a copy, courtesy of South Caroliniana Library, University of South Carolina (Samuel Latimer Papers, 22-968).*

armed citizens gathered to protect the police. The sheriff and citizens then confronted possibly one hundred armed students. When mediation failed, in a last ditch effort, leaders appealed to James Henry Thornwell, the much-beloved former president of South Carolina College who had resigned to serve as president of the Presbyterian seminary in Columbia. Thornwell addressed the crowd, promised the students that he personally would investigate their grievances and led the students in procession back to campus. En route, the students enthusiastically shouted a familiar chant: "College, College."

As a result of this incident, the South Carolina General Assembly disbanded the historic cadet corps (which had been founded at the time of Marquis de Lafayette's visit to Columbia in 1824) and seized the arms stored on the campus. College authorities expelled some students and cancelled classes for three weeks. The parents of other students withdrew their sons. A few parents, like John MacQueen, desired for their sons to stay and continue their studies. MacQueen wanted his son to graduate if he could "do so without compromising his honor or forfeiting the good will of the bright minded of his fellows." In fact, the father did not know where to send his son if the younger MacQueen could not continue his studies at South Carolina College. MacQueen's dilemma was possibly a common concern for antebellum parents. They wanted their sons to gain an education, develop important networks and protect their honor. In addition, MacQueen was highly critical of published reports that the militia had been ordered to fire on the students and that President McCay had asked laborers in Columbia to attack the students. Consequently, MacQueen wanted Thornwell to provide an honest perspective on the situation.

This so-called guardhouse rebellion was the most serious of the pre–Civil War confrontations between students and Columbia leadership. Ironically, honor was an issue in this confrontation as well. The students apparently contended that they were honor-bound to support one another regardless of the situation.

In 1858, President Augustus Baldwin Longstreet successfully faced down a student uprising. The students demanded that the college recognize John C. Calhoun's birthday as a college holiday. The president refused, and in protest, the students tarred their seats so that classes could not be held. In response, Longstreet suspended the protestors. His decisive action brought a period of peace to the South Carolina College campus. As a result, students, faculty and administration temporarily laid aside their grievances. Ironically, while the students jousted over food, drink and class attendance, major changes were on the horizon as South Carolina considered secession.

GAMBLING

Despite Columbia city ordinances banning gambling and prohibiting billiards and other gaming tables within fifteen miles of the city, many residents, including South Carolina College students, ignored the law. For some, games of chance were an essential entertainment outlet. In general, law enforcement ignored such infractions, and few were prosecuted for this vice. Those convicted and punished for gambling were usually out-of-towners, especially professional gamblers. Gambling houses offered games of chance for all socioeconomic levels. While city leaders attempted to limit gambling opportunities, the presence of South Carolina College made Columbia an attractive center for games of chance. Organizers operated with one eye open for the law. Games involving dice—such as chuck-a-luck (played with three dice) and E-O (Even-Odd), perhaps a relative of roulette or poker—were particularly popular with the undergraduates. Many a young man away from home for the first time succumbed to gaming and other attractions in South Carolina's capital city. Then as now, young undergraduates with unaccustomed freedom and resources are eager for new experiences. Many found the experience expensive. A student commented that he had found it necessary to rescue a friend who had lost not only his proverbial shirt but also his pants.

Presentments of the Richland District Grand Jury disclose continued concern about gambling and its effects on society. In 1866, the grand jury submitted a presentment about the "most prominent and alarming evil"—gambling. In addition to gaming's "fruitful and patent immorality," the jury found that gambling seduced young men and made them vulnerable to "depravity." Consequently, jury members recommended that gaming houses be licensed. The jurors argued that if the evil of gambling "had to be endured as an incubus," then it should be heavily taxed and contribute equally to the state treasury "as do honest avocations."

MURDER WILL OUT

While most criminals were nonviolent, there were exceptions, and the dark side made news in antebellum Columbia. According to the *Camden Gazette*, the death of a slave in October 1819 excited comment. Thomas T. Willison, esquire, convened an inquest into the death of Dinah, a slave of Christina Hornsby. Christina Hornsby may be the seventy-six-year-old woman enumerated on the 1850 census. At that time, she owned real estate valued at $1,500. Christina Hornsby, the widow of Henry Hornsby, owned several tracts of land (including two tracts on Crane Creek) in Richland County. When she died in 1859, her four children (James Sanders, Nathaniel, Leah Caroline and Christina) inherited her estate. According to the 1850 Census, Christina Hornsby owned fifteen slaves. The incident involving Dinah occurred about four miles north of Columbia. The jury deliberated and found "that the aforesaid Female Negro Dinah, came to her death by the violence of beating and hanging around the waist with a chain, inflicted by Christina Hornsby."

This sad story illustrates one of the little noted human costs of South Carolina's "peculiar institution."

In March 1826, Governor Richard I. Manning issued a proclamation concerning the murder of Margaret Clancy. Clancy died February 25 in the city of Columbia. The proclamation offered a reward of $200 for the "apprehension" of her husband, Thomas Clancy, the suspected villain. According to the proclamation, Thomas Clancy was between thirty-five and forty years of age, stood five feet ten or eleven inches, had dark eyes and black hair and was a stout man with a "full face."

William Gaffney was a particularly notorious murderer. Before public outrage drove him from the state in 1847, Gaffney killed at least two African Americans. In 1840, Gaffney was between forty and forty-nine years of age and head of a household that included four adult men, one adult woman, three children and twenty-two slaves. In 1844, the state surveyed 716 acres for Gaffney on Cedar Creek in Richland County. Reputedly, Gaffney sadistically enjoyed killing fellow human beings, while another lowlife named Price allegedly bludgeoned to death an old man merely as an outlet for "his rage." Psychopaths are not a new phenomenon.

But white men were not the only murderers in Columbia. In April 1846, Jacob, a slave who belonged to Captain Thomas H. Wade, murdered his wife, Silvia. Silvia was the slave of John Faust. As Silvia sat by the fire lighting her pipe, Jacob struck her in the head with an axe. Silvia died from the attack, and Jacob was arrested. Tried by a Magistrates and Freeholders Court, Jacob confessed his guilt. Based on that confession, the court sentenced him to be hanged on May 22, 1846.

To the grand jury of 1838, such bloodshed—or, as they expressed it, "frequent cases of murder & destruction of human life"—called for drastic government action. To the jurors, the root of the evil was the practice of carrying concealed weapons—a perennial concern for Americans. They considered hiding pistols and knives especially egregious. Consequently, the grand jury condemned the carrying of concealed weapons as a "dangerous and cowardly practice, which stamps disgrace upon the present ages; and although our own state stands advantageously contrasted with many others in relation to this practice; yet the grand jury are satisfied that humanity calls for some legislative action to suppress what is clearly a growing evil."

The jury also wanted legal limitations on the sale of bowie knives, dirks and "all such weapons intended for offence, and contrived to be secretly worn about the Person." In addition, the jury recommended that all cases involving the use of "such weapons" should be classified as murder and not manslaughter.

At the time of the outbreak of war, Columbia was a rail center with two depots. Houses of prostitution flourished around the railroad depots and market. Columbia's market originally operated from the ground level of town hall at the corner of Main and Gervais Streets, but by 1860, the market had moved from Main (Richardson) to the more inviting Assembly Street.

A BANK ROBBERY

In 1870, a bank robbery altered Edwin J. Scott's vacation plans. In 1870, the sixty-six-year-old Scott was a banker who possessed real estate worth $10,000 and personal property valued at $2,000. A decade earlier, Scott was the cashier for the Commercial Bank in Columbia and lived on the east corner of Pickens, opposite Washington. But in 1870, he was doing business as "Scott, Williams & Company, bankers." The bank building stood on the west side of Richardson (Main) Street between Plain (Hampton) and Washington Streets.

On Saturday, April 16, thieves broke into the vault of his bank and destroyed the "burglar-proof" safe. The thieves stole the bank's funds, special deposits and Scott's profits for two years and disdainfully left their own tools behind. Scott offered a reward for information and recovery of the money. Investigation revealed that three or four men had camped between Columbia and the river at the time of the robbery. A search of the campsite turned up a receipt with the names of J.A. Asdell and Jack Tierney. The investigation revealed that Asdell had checked into the Columbia Hotel before the robbery. Pinkerton agents identified Tierney as a person of interest in another investigation and traced him to New York City. As a result of this major financial setback, Scott had to abandon his much-anticipated trip to Europe.

In 1872, however, a Tennessee banker contacted Scott with a possible lead. A man named Smith had offered him bank bills stolen in the Columbia robbery. Scott traveled to Nashville and learned that the elusive Smith had departed for Louisville, Kentucky, though he claimed New York City as his permanent address. Sample contacted Blythe, a detective in Louisville, Kentucky, who shadowed Smith without incident during his time there. Smith continued to New York and contacted Sample again, offering Columbia Bank of Exchange bills that had been on deposit with Scott's bank at the time of the robbery. The Nashville bank agreed to the sale, and Sample headed to New York to identify Smith so New York authorities could arrest him and extradite him to South Carolina.

Scott wired the governor of South Carolina to request the needed paperwork. The governor sent the requisition by Robert C. Shiver. In 1870, Shiver, a native of North Carolina, was a thirty-one-year-old retail dry goods merchant, who owned real estate valued at $20,000 and personal property worth $15,000. The Nashville bank then sent Smith a check in care of the express office at the Maxwell Hotel. Despite hiring Pinkerton detectives to guard the office and intercept Smith, the plan sadly went awry. The man the agents intercepted claimed an alibi and threatened legal action if detained. At that point, given the circumstances, neither Shiver nor Sample or the Pinkerton men wanted the responsibility of detaining the man believed to be Smith. Shiver confided to Scott that he suspected chicanery—that is, that the real culprit had bribed an agent and escaped to Canada. Edwin Scott's long saga finally ended, as T.S. Eliot wrote, "not with a bang, but a whimper." Despite Scott's best efforts, none of the stolen funds were ever recovered.

RUM, BY GUM

In 1860, the South Carolina secession convention originally convened at First Baptist Church, Columbia. As a result, many considered South Carolina's capital city a "hotbed of secession." Secession had been in the air for years before the fatal decision. In 1850, James Burrill Angell visited Columbia and attended graduation ceremonies at South Carolina College. Angell reported that "several of the students' speeches referred to the secession of the State."

Civil War Columbia was a beacon of safety in a state that faced threats on several fronts. After the Battle of Port Royal in November 1861, federal military forces occupied Beaufort and the Sea Islands. The Union navy also blockaded the South Carolina coast. As early as 1862, state authorities—fearing an attack on Charleston—secretly ordered the evacuation of state government records from Charleston to Columbia.

Civil War–era saloon on Main Street. Illegal alcohol consumption was a problem in 1860s Columbia. *Courtesy of South Caroliniana Library, University of South Carolina (Samuel Latimer Papers, 22-968).*

Under the South Carolina Constitution of 1790, the state maintained two offices of the secretary of state—one in Charleston and one in Columbia. The Treasurer of the Lower Division also had his office in Charleston. These records were stored in a special vault in the basement of the new statehouse then under construction.

In addition to paper refugees, many Lowcountry families, like the Charles Edward Leveretts of Beaufort, fled inland as well. South Carolina banks also moved their operations to the capital city. Columbia was considered a safe haven. The Confederacy also relocated its currency operations to Columbia. In addition, the city was a center of arms manufacturing, wartime fundraising and a wayside hospital to care for wounded troops who passed through the city's two railroad depots. Visits from active duty troops galvanized local attention, while housing and food shortages plagued the capital. Those residents who could cultivated gardens to supplement their diets. Costs for basics such as flour skyrocketed as inflation devalued Confederate currency.

With such an influx of refugees and civilian and military workers, preserving law and order was a challenge. The city's police force and civic leaders faced price gouging, prostitution and bootlegging. The illegal sale of spirituous liquor was a special concern. Such concerns were not new. During the antebellum years, several grand jury presentments complained about liquor sales and retail licenses. For example, in 1841, the grand jury expressed its view that "shops and places where ardent spirits are retailed" under state license are "a great nuisance" and contribute to immorality and the destruction of "valuable citizens and families." By 1840, the temperance movement was well underway in antebellum South Carolina and many representatives and residents lobbied for stricter liquor laws and prohibition.

According to the 1860 census, there were fourteen saloons in Columbia. According to the 1860 city directory for Columbia, thirteen of the fourteen saloons were on Main Street (then known as Richardson). The fourteenth one was under the Congaree House. Three of these saloons were in hotels: the Congaree Hotel on the northwest corner of Main and Lady; the City Hotel, southwest corner of Laurel and Main; and the United States Hotel, southeast corner of Lady and Main. Alfred M. Hunt, a native of North Carolina, was the manager of the United States Hotel and Joseph A. Bartlett, the barkeeper. Samuel D. Mundle, a South Carolinian, was the barkeeper for the City Hotel, and William H. West was the restaurant manager for the Congaree Hotel. One of the saloons, Grieshaber & Wolf, also on Main Street, was a brewery and a bar. Emanuel Grieshaber, a twenty-eight-year-old native of Germany, was the brewer, and William Wolf, another young German, was the bartender. J. Bauman & Co., Columbia's other brewery, also had a Main Street address.

An advertisement sponsored by Isaac D. Mordecai in the 1860 Columbia city directory suggests the wide variety of available spirits. Mordecai, a local merchant, operated his business from a store at 28 Richardson (Main) Street. There, he offered the following selection for discerning consumers:

BRANDIES, Holland and Old Tom London GIN, Scotch, German and Old Rye WHISKEY, Old Port, Madeira, Sherry, Claret, & Champagne WINES of the best brands, BITTERS, Cherry & Blackberry BRANDY; ABSINTHE; BAY RUM, London PORTER and Scotch ALE; LAGER BEER and CHAMPAGNE CIDER, in jugs.

Thomas J. Goodwyn served as mayor or intendent of Columbia during the Civil War. *Copy of a portrait (Prints Goodwyn), courtesy of the South Caroliniana Library, University of South Carolina.*

Wartime measures to limit liquor production and sale failed. Confederate authorities wanted to conserve the corn crop for the war effort. Yet bootlegging thrived, and liquor continued to flow on Columbia's Main Street. As a further complication, alcohol for medical and other war-related needs was legally manufactured in Columbia.

During the war years, matters deteriorated. Consequently, in 1864, Thomas J. Goodwyn, mayor of Columbia, and city aldermen petitioned the South Carolina General Assembly asking that

> *their powers may be so increased and extended, at least during the present war, as to enable them more efficiently to check the increase of Vice and Crime which the unlimited sale of spirituous liquors is so well calculated to engender…*
>
> *…in pursuance of the declared policy of the State, as expressed in Various Acts of the General Assembly, refused absolutely to grant license for retailing spirituous liquors. That they have by the exercise of all the power conferred upon them, attempted to suppress its sale, within the city but regret to say their efforts have been ineffectual, and the business of retailing is now carried on to a greater extent,…than ever before in this City. The City Council of Columbia had the power to impose fines to the extent of Fifty Dollars, but if the fine exceeds twenty Dollars, execution cannot [be ordered] for its collection until suit has been brought and judgment obtained in the Court of Common Pleas. The courts being now virtually closed, the Council is practically restricted to the fine of Twenty Dollars only. This amount in Confederate Currency is so trifling, that offenders can well afford to pay, and still continue to offend.*

The easy availability of liquor was not only a perennial challenge for law enforcement in Columbia during the war years but also an important factor in one of Columbia's greatest disasters: the burning of Columbia in February 1865.

Chapter 3

Behind Closed Doors

On July 2, 1844, James Henry Hammond wrote in his diary: "the rumours [*sic*] put afloat…have been taken up by my enemies." With these cryptic remarks, Hammond obliquely addressed and dismissed a significant family scandal with long ramifications. The principals were Hammond, Wade Hampton II, John L Manning, William C. Preston and the four Hampton daughters—Harriet, Catherine, Ann and Caroline.

Hammond was an ambitious young man with limited means. His father, Elisha, was bursar for South Carolina College. While his father provided him with an education, Hammond always felt he was on the outside looking into an inaccessible world of wealth and privilege. As historian Drew Faust noted, Hammond and John C. Calhoun had much in common. Both were planter onlookers who successfully married into the Carolina aristocracy and had dreams of political success. Hammond became a successful lawyer and editor but craved entry into South Carolina's power elite. For that, he needed land and slaves; he needed to join the plantation aristocracy. Consequently, he courted and married a wealthy, young, fatherless heiress. In 1829, Hammond met and charmed fifteen-year-old Catherine Fitzsimmons. Catherine had inherited several plantations near the Savannah River from her father. Despite her family's objections, Hammond and the heiress married in 1831. With marriage, Hammond gained access to his wife's plantations and slaves. He also gained entry to the society of influential South Carolinians. For example, in 1817, his wife's older sister, Ann (1797–1833), married Wade Hampton II (1791–1858). Hampton, a prominent planter, belonged to the influential Hampton family and had served as aide to General Andrew Jackson at New Orleans in 1815. Ann and Wade Hampton were the parents of eight children: Wade Hampton III (1818–1902), Christopher Fitzsimmons Hampton (1821–1886), Harriet Flud Hampton (1823–1848), Catherine P. Hampton (1824–1916), Ann M. Hampton (1826–1914), Caroline Louise Hampton (1828–1902), Frank Hampton (1829–1863) and Mary Fisher Hampton (1833–1866).

With marriage, Hammond abandoned law and took his new bride to Silver Bluff to manage her inheritance—over ten thousand acres of land and almost 150 slaves. Hammond became a planter interested in scientific agriculture and committed to improving his property.

James Henry Hammond, South Carolina governor and United States Senator, had a scandalous relationship with his wife's nieces. *Julian Vannerson, photographer, LC-DIG-ppmsca-26689, Courtesy of the Library of Congress.*

Within a few years, he had successfully mastered the agricultural lifestyle and wanted new horizons to conquer. Politics appealed to him. Pursuing a political career, Hammond was elected to the United States House of Representatives and, in 1835, moved his wife and four young sons from Barnwell District to Washington, D.C. Forced to resign his seat due to ill health, the Hammonds toured Europe before returning to Silver Bluff.

Though glad to be home, Hammond's ambitions were alive and well. In 1842, Hammond continued his political achievements and became governor of South Carolina. Unfortunately for future events, his long-suffering wife had just given birth to a daughter and was unable to accompany her husband to Columbia. Leaving his wife to recuperate, Hammond proceeded to Columbia, located and began decorating an appropriate house for his family. Volunteering to assist him with decorating were his wife's nieces—the four teenaged Hampton daughters. Their mother had died in 1833, and they apparently were entranced with the charismatic Hammond. According to his accounts, the young women tempted him "beyond endurance." Rather than flee or summon an older woman to supervise his time with them, Hammond, by his own admission, engaged in a variety of sexual activities—stopping only at intercourse. One of the daughters told her father what "Uncle James" had proposed and perhaps done, and Hampton vowed revenge. Rather than fight a duel with another gentleman, though, Hampton had a different idea.

As Hammond wrote in his diary, "An unfortunate rupture with Hampton just before the [legislative] Session terminated my relations with him and his whole family, including Manning and the Prestons." Hammond cited the "rupture" in his relationship with Hampton as the reason he packed up his family and left Columbia. In 1844, James Henry Hammond, unaware at the time of Hampton's plans, completed his term as governor, expecting, at any moment to receive a challenge from Hampton. When a challenge did not come, the relieved Hammond left for Silver Bluff expecting the situation to blow over.

The Hammonds reached their Beech Island plantation on January 1, 1844. The "rupture" not only made him an outcast with his wife's family, but also ended, at least temporarily, his dream of serving in the United States Senate. Rather than issuing a challenge, Wade Hampton II, at the expense of his daughters' reputations, shared specifics of the situation and drew the proverbial line in the sand.

In his diary, Hammond conceded that he had "been wrong in the matter—the result of impulse, not design." Yet he struggled with a desire to air his perspective and vindicate himself. He feared it would "embarrass me through life." Privately, he admitted improper relations with the four Hampton daughters, ages thirteen through nineteen, but he still thought himself more wronged than wrong. As with many in similar situations, Hammond exonerated his actions at the expense of his victims. In nineteenth-century South Carolina, the expense was high. As a result of the scandal, none of the Hampton daughters married.

As punishment, Wade Hampton II attempted to use his influence and family connections to interrupt Hammond's political career. To Hampton, anyone who supported Hammond was his enemy. As the South Carolina General Assembly elected the state's United States Senators, Hammond as the outgoing governor had expectations in 1844. Nevertheless, Hampton circulated materials documenting Hammond's perfidy, although at the cost of his daughters' reputations, and Hammond lost his bid for the United States Senate. For thirteen years, there were other possibilities and other

Wade Hampton Monument with Trinity Episcopal Church (now Cathedral). General Wade Hampton III was the son of Wade Hampton II, who was a political foe of James Henry Hammond. Asheville Postcard Company, Asheville, North Carolina. *Collection of the author.*

disappointments. Hammond's political aspirations looked bleak. Those years were not only difficult ones for Hammond's public career but also challenging ones for Hammond as a family man.

Despite his growing family and attentive wife, according to historian Carol Bleser, Hammond had a "roving eye." His diaries reflect an avid appreciation of attractive women and document his liaisons with at least two of his female slaves, a mother and her daughter. Such activity was not that uncommon among southern slave owners, but the duration of Hammond's affairs distressed his wife. Eventually, Catherine Hammond, who had supported Hammond during the great scandal involving her nieces and even the relationship with the first mistress, reached a breaking point. When Hammond refused to end the relationship with the younger slave, his wife left and lived apart from him for several years. The separation and eventual reconciliation demonstrate some of the strains on the marriage of Catherine Fitzsimmons and James Henry Hammond.

Finally, in 1857, he achieved his goal—a seat in the United States Senate. There, he spoke passionately about the importance of cotton and the necessity of "mud-sills"—(slaves) to the success of civilization. For example, in the United States Senate on March 4, 1858, Hammond said:

In all social systems there must be a class to do the menial duties, to perform the drudgery of life. That is, a class requiring but a low order of intellect and but little skill. Its requisites are vigor, docility, fidelity. Such a class you must have, or you would not have that other class which leads progress, civilization, and refinement. It constitutes the very mud-sill of society… Fortunately for the South, she found a race adapted to that purpose…and [we] *call them slaves.*

In 1860, James Henry Hammond owned real estate worth $30,000 and personal property (including his slaves) valued at $40,000. He lived with his wife and children in his recently completed home, Redcliffe, on Beech Island in Edgefield District.

Yet despite his many accomplishments and worldly success, few have addressed Hammond's fondness for young women. For example, he courted his future wife at age fifteen and married her at seventeen. He began a relationship with his slave mistress's daughter when she was only a child of twelve, and he, by his own admission, engaged in improper activities with the Hampton daughters, ages thirteen to nineteen. Such a track record should raise major questions about Hammond's sexual preferences.

Chapter 4

Ladies of the Evening

The old adage about prostitution being the world's oldest occupation has a certain resonance for South Carolina's capital. Perhaps the city's early dependence on the legislative session with few permanent residents created a legacy of itinerancy and impermanence—similar to a frontier town. Boardinghouses and hotels catered to the seasonal visitors. Hospitality services included livery, stables, bootblacks, mercantile, restaurants, laundries, shoeshine operations and prostitution. The tradition of providing female "comfort" became a byword for Columbia, establishing a tradition that, despite major efforts at eradication (some of which will be discussed later), continues to the present. According to Edwin Scott, on occasion, Democrat and Whig candidates hired women from Columbia's "Holy Land" to entertain potential voters.

By 1860, the Columbia city market had moved to Assembly Street, and the two railroad depots on Gervais were major anchors for development in Columbia. Such activity attracted locals and visitors and such entertainment options as boardinghouses, restaurants, taverns and houses of prostitution.

In 1860, according to the United States Census, at least two women in Columbia indicated that they operated "house[s] of ill fame." One was Margaret Kelly, a twenty-year-old South Carolina native, who owned personal property valued at $200. In addition to Kelly, the following individuals lived in her residence: Elizabeth Wilson (age twenty-six), Jane Cook (age twenty), Eliza W. Cook (age three), John Cook (age six months),

View of Columbia looking southwest from the capital, 1865. Columbia's red-light district lay southwest of the statehouse. From *Art Work Scenes in South Carolina, 1895. Courtesy of South Caroliniana Library, University of South Carolina.*

Frankie Cook (age five), Joseph Cook (age ten) and William Brown (age sixteen). All were South Carolina natives. The other proprietor was Rosa (Rose) L. Grant (Le Grand). Grant, forty years old, was born in Germany and possessed personal property valued at $800. Residents of her house were Amelia Brown (twenty-one years old and a native of New York), Mary Jones (twenty years old and a native of New York), Blanche Mellville (age nineteen and a native of South Carolina), Kateline Seabrook (eighteen years of age and also born in South Carolina), Julia Seabrook (an eighteen-year-old native of Georgia) and Florence Johnston (age sixteen and another native of Georgia).

Kelly operated a house in a multiracial working-class neighborhood. The occupations of her neighbors included seamstress, carpenter, shoemaker, engineer and wheelwright. Few owned their homes. Grant's enterprise perhaps served a different clientele. Her neighbors were generally property owners and included schoolteachers and a Methodist clergyman. Near her residence was the Columbia Orphanage. According to Columbia historian John Hammond Moore, Grant, nicknamed "Dutch Rose," was the "best known madam" in the city. Grant's establishment stood on the southwest corner of Gates (Park) and Lady Streets.

Grant's murder in 1863 was a *cause célèbre*. According to Moore, Thaddeus Saunders, a native of Virginia, was the culprit. Saunders may be the ten-year-old Thaddeus S. Saunders enumerated in 1850 living with his parents, Alvin G. and Alley Saunders, in Richmond, Virginia.

His father was a teacher. Once a scout for Confederate hero Thomas J. "Stonewall" Jackson, while on leave, Saunders visited Columbia in the summer of 1863. During that visit, the inebriated Saunders decided to rob Grant. With an accomplice, he drugged and strangled her. She survived long enough to identify her attackers.

Although he fled the scene, Saunders was eventually captured in Alabama and returned to Columbia, where he was tried and convicted. While awaiting execution, Saunders converted to Catholicism and Father J.J. O'Connell of St. Peter's actively lobbied for his release. In 1848, O'Connell became pastor of St. Peter's Catholic Church. O'Connell thought highly of Saunders and his potential. Despite a temporary stay of execution, Saunders was executed in June 1864. In a macabre twist, authorities ordered an exhumation of the body. Rumors on the street alleged that Saunders had somehow survived his hanging. General Wade Hampton III and other prominent citizens witnessed the exhumation, and the body in the grave was Saunders. Hampton later served as governor of South Carolina and United States senator. O'Connell and the sheriff of Richland County published an open invitation for city residents to attend Saunders's funeral—an unusual twist for an unusual story.

The 1860 census data offers a window on a generally clandestine, or at least ignored, enterprise. Yet it is doubtful that Columbia—with a population of 8,052 in 1860—had only two houses of prostitution. When Columbia burned in February 1865, one of the early fires broke out in the brothels

"Millwood," Ruins of plantation home of General Wade Hampton. Photo by Sargeant, Graycraft Card Company, Danville, Virginia. *Collection of the author.*

Office of the South Carolina Railroad on Gervais Street after the 1865 fire. Carte-de-viste by Richard Wearn, 1865. *Courtesy of South Caroliniana Library, University of South Carolina (photographs Wearn 14).*

near Gervais Street. That fire was extinguished without significant property damage. Columbia's main business district, along Richardson (Main) Street, was not as fortunate. The fire did not dampen trade. In 1866, the state prosecuted William McGinnis for "unlawfully maintaining a disorderly house." The 1860 census listed a William McGinnis, age thirteen, who listed his occupation as barkeeper.

ELLEN VOGEL

In 1883, one of Columbia's better-known "ladies" died. According to the 1879–1880 city directory of Columbia, Ellen Vogel resided at No. 59 on the east side of Senate Street. The 1880 census listed Vogel as a thirty-year-old mulatto and her occupation as "prostitute." According to the census, Vogel lived alone. Ill at the time, Vogel, born in Louisiana, wrote her will on March 10, 1883. C.H. Monroe, Mary Sweeney and Frank Green witnessed Vogel's will. She died shortly thereafter, as John Bauskett, her executor, filed to administer her estate on March 19, 1883. In 1876, Bauskett practiced with Walter S. Monteith, with offices in the law range on the east side of Washington Street. By 1888, Bauskett was an attorney and United States Commissioner. His office was at 124½ Richardson (Main) and his residence stood on the east corner of Taylor and Henderson Streets.

In her will, Vogel made a number of bequests and expressed her desire to be buried in Randolph Cemetery. She requested her executor to purchase a lot and erect an iron fence and marble stone. Among those bequests were several to the Reverend B.B. Babbitt, her "spiritual advisor" for his "mission and charitable work in Columbia" and to purchase a communion service for St. Luke's Episcopal Church, then under construction in Columbia. Babbit, according to the Columbia city directory of 1875–76, was professor of natural and mechanical philosophy and astronomy at the University of South Carolina. She also left funds to acquire a bell for Wesleyan Methodist Episcopal Church in Columbia, where Reverend Pinckney was pastor.

Vogel owned two lots with houses on Senate Street. She left the lot and house at 100 Senate Street to her godchild, Eleanor Burke. Burke, who also received other bequests, was the granddaughter of Anna Burke and, according to Vogel, "is sometimes called Helen Henderson." In addition, Vogel designated funds to purchase a home for Samuel Richardson and his wife, Christiana, in "payment of any and all services." She made cash gifts to Diana Bollen, Anna Burke, Harriet Kennedy and Harriet Johnson. Vogel specified furniture and china bequests for Cecilia Richardson, Eleanor Burke, Emma Toland and Mary Rose. She also asked that the following women—Anna Burke, Eleanor Burke, May Burke, Allie Burke, Diana Bollen, Christina Richardson and Harriet Johnson—share her clothing.

Ellen Vogel acknowledged an "estrangement between me and my relations." As a result, she "knowingly left them nothing" in her will. She frequently described her bequests as an acknowledgement of the individual's kindness and assistance to her. Vogel also designated gifts of furniture for Alice Duvall Green, the infant daughter of Dr. Frank Green, and of jewelry to Mrs. John Stanley and her daughters. As Vogel notes, she honored the Stanleys "on account of kindness received" from Mrs. Carrington, the mother of Mrs. John Stanley. Vogel left a silver tea set to H.L. Johnson, "editor or proprietor of the *Hillsdale Herald*" in Hillsdale, New York. Her residuary legatee was Captain W.B. Stanley.

Vogel's beneficiaries were an interesting cross-section of Columbia residents. Frank Green was a physician. His office was at 14 on the east side of Plain (Hampton) Street, while he lived at 40 Gervais Street. The city directory for 1875–76 lists only one individual named Carrington— Charles V. Carrington, who was the secretary and auditor of the Greenville and Columbia Railroad. Carrington lived at 23 on the west side of Plain (Hampton). The legatee named Samuel Richardson may be the Samuel Richardson who lived at 97 Gates (Park) Street. In 1880, Samuel Richardson, a native of South Carolina, was thirty-eight years old. His wife, Christina, was only nineteen years old. The couple had a six-month-old daughter named Annie. The Richardson household also included Charles Bowling (age five), a brother in law and Delilah Chapman (age seventy-five).

Benjamin B. Babbitt (1828–1888) was not only a university professor but also an Episcopal minister who had moved from New York to Columbia to establish a mission. In an effort to find competent faculty members who were acceptable to Republican leadership, the trustees appointed Babbitt to his chair in 1871. Babbitt also served as chair of the university faculty from 1873 to 1875. In 1870, Babbitt, a native of Rhode Island, lived in Bristol, Rhode Island, with his family and perhaps his mother, Abby Babbitt, age sixty-one. On April 5, 1865, Benjamin Bosworth Babbitt preached a sermon on the death of Walter L. Raymond, a Union soldier, who died in a Confederate prison at Salisbury. As Babbitt notes, the young man died "for God and my country." Babbitt preached the sermon at Christ Church, Andover, Massachusetts.

H.L. Johnson, the other New York connection, is more difficult to locate. But the *Hillsdale Herald* first appeared in 1879 with E.J. Beardsley as publisher.

Despite Ellen Vogel's wishes, Bauskett, the executor, informed the probate court in April 1883 that the estate's debts exceeded available funds. As a result, on April 11, 1883, the court granted Bauskett permission to sell Vogel's personal property. According to the inventory and appraisal of Ellen Vogel's estate, the appraisers, L.T. Levin, Andrew Lee and J. B. Pollock, valued her personal property at $1,002.61—not enough to fund her bequests.

The inventory of Vogel's personal property offers an unusual glimpse into the world of a successful courtesan. At the time of her death, Vogel lived in a six-room house that included a kitchen, dining room, passageway, a northwest room, a northeast room, a southeast front room and a southwest front room. Her kitchen, in addition to the expected equipment, had three birdcages and an ice cream churn. Among the furnishings of the dining room were several mahogany tables, six chairs, a wardrobe, carpet, two screens, twenty plates and a wide variety of dishes, pitchers, salt cellars, serving dishes, a decanter, tea pot, mosquito nets and an hourglass. The northeast room was a bedroom whose furnishings included a bed, bureau, rocker, wardrobe, table, chairs, curtains and cornices. The passageway that apparently separated the northeast and northwest rooms had a sideboard, pictures, carpets and doormats. The northwest room was another bedroom with a bed, window shades, curtains, cornices, tin chamber set, washstand with three basins and a pitcher and a towel rack. The furnishings of the southeast front room included a wardrobe, two washstands, bureau, sofa, two rockers, a whatnot, two beds, six feather pillows, a china chamber set, cornices and shades, two toilette sets, lamps and a call bell.

From its furnishings, the southwest front room held Vogel's wardrobe. Listed are black watered silk, blue silk, brown silk, velvet, black cashmere, black satin and "maroon diagonal" dresses. Vogel also owned a brocade suit, India silk suit, a silk poplin suit, a blue brocade suit, a brocade cloak, three hoop skirts, a bustle, corset and "appurtenances for Hair dressing." In addition, she had a muff, lace and cashmere shawls and bonnets.

INTO THE TWENTIETH CENTURY

While later census entries are not as noticeably forthcoming, other sources document this aspect of city life. For example, according to the Columbia city directory of 1905, Ella Parnell, who lived at 1105 Gates Street, listed her occupation as "madame." According to the 1900 census, Ella Parnell, age eighteen, was born in North Carolina in July 1881. In 1900, she boarded on Gates Street with Nelly Mitchell (age twenty-five) and another boarder, Margaret Lundsden (twenty-two years old). All three women listed their occupations as dressmaker.

More than prostitution concerned Columbians in the early twentieth century. Vice and villainy flourished in the new century.

Chapter 5

War on Vice

Part I/World War I

The outbreak of the Great War—or the War to End All Wars—changed lives for tens of thousands of Americans. Gearing up for the war effort, many young men from rural areas encountered city life for the first time. This interface became an issue for Columbia and Richland County. The influx of draftees to Camp Jackson strained military-civilian relations. Prior to World War I, Columbia licensed houses of ill fame and kept them isolated within a set zone—in fact, the same area where similar businesses existed before the Civil War.

Racketing up the pressure, in June 1917, Secretary of War Newton D. Baker warned Mayor Lewis A. Griffith that the United States would not tolerate a "segregated district of vice" near Camp Jackson. As a last resort, he threatened to remove the camp if vice and liquor enforcement did not improve. At present, officials had set a five-mile zone around the camp. Within that zone, prostitution was strictly prohibited. Notwithstanding, military officials wanted more. They insisted on no contained "tenderloin district" within access of Camp Jackson.

While city attorney C.S. Monteith drafted an ordinance in July, there were conflicting opinions about the problem.

The proposed ordinance provided:
Section 1. That it shall be unlawful for any person or persons to maintain, keep, live at or frequent a disorderly house or bawdy house within the limits of the city of Columbia.

This 1915 skyline view of Columbia shows hotels, churches and the YMCA, as well as the Palmetto Building, the National Loan and Exchange Building (Berringer Building) and the Carolina National Bank Building. *Courtesy of South Caroliniana Library, University of South Carolina (Postcards rich co 652).*

First recruits enter Camp Jackson. *Courtesy of South Caroliniana Library, University of South Carolina (Postcards rich co 155).*

Section 2. That it shall be unlawful for any person or persons to rent or let, whether himself or by agent or whether he be principal or agent, any house within the limits of the city of Columbia when he has reason to believe that the same is being rented or let for the purpose of maintaining therein a disorderly house or bawdy house, or to permit any property that he may own or have in charge as agent to be used for the purpose of maintaining therein a disorderly house or bawdy house...

Section 3. That a bawdy house or disorderly house shall be construed to mean a house to which persons resort for the purpose of immoral sexual relations or prostitution whether the same be a house in which prostitutes or persons of evil fame live or a house of assignation.

Other sections addressed other contingencies and the penalty for violating the conditions of the ordinance. Anyone convicted of violating this ordinance was guilty of a misdemeanor and would be fined $1,000 or sentenced to serve "on the public works of the city, or to be imprisoned not exceeding 30 days."

"THE RED LIGHT STILL BURNS"

Columbia needed the military, so, effective August 1, a city ordinance closed the houses of prostitution. Officials conducted an inventory of the houses and their residents. The inventory listed the residents of the white establishments but not of the black-run houses. The survey of the working women listed working names, real names, ages, years in the business, years in Columbia, number of children and if they wanted to leave the business or continue as a prostitute. The inventory also listed the addresses of the houses, the owner of the property and if the operator rented the house, the amount of the rent and the board paid by the inhabitants of the house. The houses stood on Gates (now Park), College, Wheat, Senate, Lincoln and Pendleton Streets. Thirteen of the ninety-eight women were listed as "madams." Among the madams were Bettie Booth (Pearl Burnett), Marcella Dutrow, Stella Johnson, Queenie Marion, Frances Morgan, Ethel McCann, Nellie Mitchell, Lula Only, Minnie Rivers, Camille Rose, Minnie Spigner, Dallas Starnes, Edna Smith, Alma Williams, Irene Whiteside, Anne Grayer, Lessie Bryant and Carrie Foster.

Rehabilitation was an option, but few of the women were interested. Since 1907, the Reverend J.M. Pike had operated the Door of Hope, an outreach ministry for prostitutes interested in pursuing a different lifestyle. Pike testified that in 1917, despite the ministry's efforts, the number of prostitutes in Columbia had not changed from 1897. As attorney Alan Johnstone Jr. asserted, "Breaking up the segregated district is the first step in ridding the city of vice…But none of us thinks that merely closing the district will put an end to the matter."

Insurance commissioner F.H. McMaster commented on the flagrant behavior of Columbia prostitutes when he first moved to Columbia. As a

Gervais and Park Street sign, the Vista. Gervais and Park Streets marked two boundaries for Columbia's infamous "tenderloin" district. *Photograph by Jacob H. Helsley.*

The camp is a small city of 40,000 men. The Barracks are grouped about a parade ground. Each Barracks contains a company of 200 men and there are about 200 buildings just like those shown in the picture in the Cantonment and in all the camps there are 5,000 all built on exactly the same specifications. There are in all over 1,000 buildings in the Camp including hospitals, officers' quarters, stores, Y. M. C. A. buildings, headquarters buildings, etc.

U.S. Army cantonment, Camp Jackson, South Carolina. *Courtesy of South Caroliniana Library, University of South Carolina (Postcards rich co 416 os).*

young man, he remembered paying twenty-five or fifty cents for admission to the old Columbia Theatre and seeing "with revulsion sitting haughtily in boxes, low breasted whitened beauties which no manager of a respectable theatre would tolerate now." He also remembered prostitutes driving around the university campus. "But the red flag of invitation still waves, the red light still burns."

The Reverend Kirkman Finlay of Trinity Church (now Cathedral) supported passage of the ordinance. As he noted, "A committee of noble women of the city has recently visited all of these houses and found that the inmates were expecting to close up and move." Finlay thought it would be helpful to end the suspense and set a date.

VICE ON POINT

Power players convened on August 31, 1917, to develop ways to control vice in Columbia and around Camp Jackson. Those attending were Mayor Griffith; Sheriff McCain; Chief of Police J.W. Richardson; Colonel Edwin Bell, provost marshal for Camp Jackson; Starling, police; Colin S. Monteith, city attorney; E.M. DuPre, city council; Alan Johnstone; and Walter Clarke. Penalties for violating city ordinances included a fine of $1,000 or twelve months in jail, or both, for operating a brothel and a similar punishment for selling liquor near the base.

On September 26, 1917, Colonel Edwin Bell angrily asserted that a lawyer who used all legal means at his disposal to "turn loose upon the community an infected prostitute" was "worse than a battalion of Germans." Bell was meeting with community leaders to discuss issues of prostitution and liquor access in Columbia. According to Bell, Columbia was doing a better job controlling liquor sales than prostitution. Apparently, hotel porters were the main source of illicit liquor sales to servicemen. Current efforts were successful in limiting the trade. Controlling prostitution in Columbia was a different matter.

Bell reported that there were sixty ladies of the evening in Columbia, and between ten and twelve were walking the streets each evening. Bell blamed a lack of enforcement, asserting that the "majority of the soldiers here are good clean fellows," so he was incensed to "think of some of them being incapacitated, being thus transported to France to consume food, to occupy hospital space and use up medicines, so badly needed by those who are fighting for their country." Bell cited the costs to the war effort of seventy-seven thousand infected allied soldiers.

A major factor in the sex trade was the use of taxis (transport vehicles). Bell alleged that "certain of these automobile drivers had photographs

Right: MPs, Camp Jackson, North Columbia Camp, by Griffith Photo, Columbia, circa 1918. *Courtesy of South Caroliniana Library, University of South Carolina (Photographs 15068 panorama).*

Opposite, middle: The Columbia, February 25, 1907. Porters at Columbia hotels allegedly steered eager consumers to prostitutes, games of chance and blind tigers. *Courtesy of South Caroliniana Library, University of South Carolina (Postcards rich co 452).*

Opposite, bottom: Governor's Mansion, Columbia. Asheville Post Card Company, Asheville, North Carolina. *Collection of the author.*

Right: World War Memorial, University of South Carolina, corner of Sumter and Pendleton Streets. Curteich-Chicago "C.T. Art-Colortone" Post Card. *Collection of the author.*

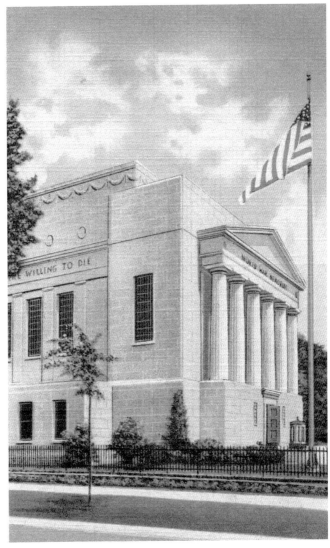

of prostitutes which they would show…their patrons" and then arrange contact. In the future, these vehicles would not be allowed to transport soldiers to and from Camp Jackson. Completion of Trenholm Road would make this surveillance easier. Guards would intercept the taxis and require the passengers to disembark and walk the two miles or so to base.

Regardless, Bell saw progress and predicted that shortly Columbia would "be freer from vice and liquor selling than ever before in its history."

In November 1916, Governor Richard I. Manning forwarded a telegram from Newton D. Baker, United States Secretary of War, to the mayors of all South Carolina towns with military installations. That communique emphasized the need for continued "vigilance" against prostitution and liquor sales "until demobilization is fully accomplished." The affected South Carolina towns were Columbia, Charleston, Greenville and Spartanburg. As the secretary of war asserted, "The war department is determined to return the soldiers to their families and to civil life uncontaminated by disease."

Chapter 6

Boys Will Be Boys

S outh Carolina College closed during the Civil War. Students and many of the faculty enlisted. Following the war, the college reopened as the University of South Carolina. The integrated institution suffered during Reconstruction as white students boycotted the state's flagship institution. Closed again, the institution flourished under Bourbon governors like Wade Hampton III, and by the 1880s, it was a highly regarded state institution. Severely weakened by Governor Benjamin Tillman's attacks and lingering prejudice, the school limped into the twentieth century.

Even with great challenges ahead, in 1896 the university launched one of the greatest sport rivalries in history. On Thursday, November 12, football teams from South Carolina and Clemson played their first football game. The teams met at the fairgrounds on Elmwood. Admission was only twenty-five cents, but rain interrupted the later quarters of the game. While the Carolina team won the initial contest by a score of 12–6, the Clemson teams rebounded and claimed victory in the following four games.

THREE STRIKES?

Despite the great Clemson-Carolina football rivalry, it was the baseball team that produced fireworks in 1897. A series of misadventures pitted the Carolina team against the state militia. On May 28, 1897, the unsuspecting

Above: South Caroliniana Library, Horseshoe, University of South Carolina. Columbia Cigar & Tobacco Company. *Collection of the author.*

Left: John Gary Watts, South Carolina adjutant general, interrupted a University of South Carolina baseball game in 1897. (Prints Watts). *Courtesy of South Caroliniana Library, University of South Carolina.*

college team convened on the athletic field for a game with the Columbia Independent Fire Company. Play was disrupted when two militia companies showed up for drill and inspection by the South Carolina adjutant general, a man named John Gary Watts.

The militia had missed its approved date (May 26), but the adjutant general thought his responsibilities trumped a mere athletic outing. A temporary compromise ensued, with the militia drilling on one end of the field and the baseball teams playing on the other. A line drive that went foul quickly ended this arrangement. The ball struck one of the staff horses, and Watts ordered his troops to clear the field. In the resulting conflict, a professor and a student were injured. The *Edgefield Advertiser* criticized Watts as "entirely too bellicose" for peacetime. A military investigation found that Watts demonstrated a "serious lack of judgment."

Garnet and Orange

By 1900, football had surpassed baseball as the most popular campus sport. In 1902, Clemson and South Carolina once again played during the state fair. The underdog home team—South Carolina—scored an upset victory that triggered violent clashes between the fans. Given the rivalry, a local merchant had decorated his downtown store with Clemson and South Carolina colors and exhibits. The South Carolina exhibit featured, according to historian Daniel Hollis, a transparency showing "a gamecock crowing over a dejected tiger."

Following the great win, South Carolina students claimed the transparency and jubilantly paraded it on Main Street. A parade of the victorious team's supporters was customary. However, high spirits and high words led to clashes between Clemson cadets (Clemson was a military school until 1955) and South Carolina students. The transparency became the focus of controversy when Clemson students vowed to capture and destroy it if South Carolina students displayed it during a parade scheduled for Friday.

Despite overtures urging compliance, with the support of Christie Benet, a local attorney who also helped coach the football team, the South Carolina players refused. They defiantly paraded the transparency in the victory parade. Clemson's cadets also marched in the parade. Dismissed after the parade near the statehouse, cadets armed with swords and bayonets surged toward the Horseshoe to capture the transparency. About thirty poorly armed South Carolina students huddled behind a makeshift barricade to oppose the

Main Street from behind Confederate Monument. In 1902, Clemson
students released from parade formation rushed to the University
horseshoe. Photographed by Curtiss B. Munn, c. 1951. *Courtesy of South
Caroliniana Library, University of South Carolina (Photographs 1291-24).*

Clemson onslaught. Benet attempted to mediate the conflict and, despite early
setbacks, successfully stalled until help arrived. In the end, Columbia police
and faculty from both colleges saved the day. With peace restored, the only
casualty was the transparency—burned to seal the peace.

Still the controversy refused to die. Some alleged that Clemson cadets
had struck unarmed South Carolina students with their swords, to which
Clemson supporters rejoined that the cadet officers were acting in self-
defense as the Carolina students were armed with brass knuckles. In the
end, the university suspended the annual game. Not until 1909 did Clemson
and the University of South Carolina football teams play again. To historian
Hollis, this confrontation helped establish the gamecock as the symbol of the
University of South Carolina.

Chapter 7

Death in the Street

The Gonzales family was an American success story made up of equal parts Cuban revolutionary and South Carolina Lowcountry. The progenitor of this story was Ambrosio Jose Gonzales (1818–1892), a Cuban educator and revolutionary. He attended school in New York with P.G.T. Beauregard, and the two became friends. Pierre Gustave Toutant Beauregard (1818–1893), a native of Louisiana, was a Confederate general. As commander of Confederate forces in Charleston, Beauregard oversaw the attack on Fort Sumter on April 12, 1861, the opening shot of the Civil War.

Following his time in New York, Gonzales graduated from the University of Havana. He worked to overthrow Spanish control of Cuba and visited the United States to garner support for Cuban annexation. Possibilities for independence dimmed, so Gonzales remained in the States and became an American citizen. In 1856, the thirty-eight-year-old Gonzales married the sixteen-year-old Harriott Rutledge Elliott. Disappointed in his business efforts, Gonzales moved his wife and children to Cuba. After the untimely death of his young wife, Gonzales returned with his six children to South Carolina. In 1891, three of his sons—Ambrose Elliott, Narciso Gener and William Elliott Gonzales—founded the *State* newspaper in Columbia.

The Gonzales brothers were supporters of Judge Alexander Cheves Haskell, who served as the first president of the State Company. A.C. Haskell (1839–1910), a graduate of South Carolina College, enlisted in Confederate service and in 1864 was named colonel of the Seventh South Carolina Cavalry.

Haskell led Democratic Party efforts to regain control of South Carolina in 1876 and helped elect General Wade Hampton governor. In 1877, Hampton named Haskell to the South Carolina Supreme Court. In 1890, Haskell fervently opposed Benjamin Tillman's gubernatorial candidacy. Tillman ridiculed Hampton, Haskell and other Bourbon leaders and waged an openly racist campaign. Unsuccessful in defeating Tillman's nomination, Haskell mounted a rival Democratic ticket to oppose Tillman in the general election. Tillman won, but Haskell then worked with the Gonzales brothers to organize the *State*. The newspaper and its editors kept a keen and critical eye on Tillman and his policies. At the time of his death on April 23, 1910, Haskell was vice-president of the National Loan & Exchange Bank of Columbia.

Ambrose Gonzales was the publisher and N.G. Gonzales the first editor of the newspaper. Under his leadership, the paper actively opposed

Above: Alexander Cheves Haskell, judge and Confederate veteran, was the first president of the State Company. Engraved by F.B. Kernan in *Cyclopedia of Eminent and Representative Men of the Carolinas,* Nineteenth Century, Vol. 1 (Prints Haskell). *Courtesy of South Caroliniana Library, University of South Carolina.*

Left: N.G. Gonzales, pioneering South Carolina newspaper editor who, with his brothers, founded the State. Copy of a photograph, by Reckling & Sons, Columbia. *Courtesy of South Caroliniana Library, University of South Carolina (Photographs 4101-1).*

Benjamin "Pitchfork Ben" Tillman and his supporters. Also, as Ambrose later wrote, the *State* was the first paper in the South to attack the barbarity of lynching. The editors also campaigned for child labor laws and compulsory education. Given such a progressive agenda, it is no wonder that the editors were lightning rods for controversy.

"CRIME OF THE CENTURY"

On January 13, 1903, Gonzales went to work as usual and dictated an editorial entitled, "Reciprocity with Cuba." At noon, he walked to the statehouse and at 1:30 p.m. returned to review the typescript of his editorial before leaving the office to walk home for lunch. As he neared the corner of Gervais Street, he exchanged greetings with a number of individuals. But Gonzales never reached the corner. Around 2:00 p.m., he encountered James Hammond Tillman (1868–1911) at the intersection of Gervais and Main Streets. There, in front of the statehouse and onlookers, without speaking, Lieutenant Governor Tillman pulled a pistol and shot the unarmed Gonzales. Gonzales was rushed to Columbia Hospital. In critical condition, he lingered for four days before dying on January 17, 1903.

According to the Charleston *News and Courier*,

> *The shooting occurred on Main street, just at the intersection of Gervais street, in full view of the State capitol. It was an awful tragedy in broad daylight and upon the most frequented street and corner in Columbia...*
>
> *The office of* The State *is on the same block as the scene of the shooting and it took but a few moments for a great throng to assemble in front of the newspaper office...*
>
> *Policeman Roland immediately after the shooting arrested Lieut. Gov. Tillman and took him to police headquarters where he was relieved of two pistols—the one with which he shot Editor Gonzales and second large revolver of 28 calibre...*

The previous August, Gonzales had been a vocal critic of James Hammond Tillman's primary bid for governor. In print, he had called Tillman a "debauchee," "blackguard," "criminal" and "liar." Among other exposes, Gonzales had documented Tillman's carelessness with truth (he had falsified records of the South Carolina Senate) and misuse of public funds, including the

Edgefield Confederate monument fund. Tillman was known for his drinking and arrogance. Nevertheless, since the primary on August 26, 1902, Gonzales had said nothing about Tillman in print, except to publish the results of the primary.

The shooting was unprovoked and unexpected. Since the legislative session convened, Gonzales and Tillman had frequently passed each other on the street and in the statehouse without comment or altercation. Yet, "Tillman opened fire, wiped his pistol on his coat sleeve, took aim as if to fire a second time changed his mind and let his pistol fall to his side." Tillman deliberately shot the unarmed Gonzales. The stunned Gonzales then looked at Tillman and exclaimed, "Shoot again, you coward." As Gonzales fell, James Sims and Gamewell LaMotte rushed to catch him. They assisted him to the nearby newspaper office. In his office, Gonzales rested his head "on a bundle of newspapers" and asked for his wife. Several doctors rushed to his side. Unfortunately, the wound in his abdomen was so serious that surgery was Gonzales's only hope for survival.

On advice of counsel, Tillman initially refused to comment on the shooting, but the dying Gonzales was a journalist to the end. While awaiting transport to the hospital, he insisted on answering all questions. During Gonzales's ordeal, the *State* refused to comment on the incident. Rather, it reprinted stories from the Charleston *News and Courier*. While South Carolinians awaited Gonzales's fate, Tillman met with his lawyers in the county jail. Due perhaps to his connections, Tillman had a private room in the jail and even had it outfitted with his own furniture. At that point, Tillman's legal team included Congressman George W. Croft, Judge O.W. Buchanan and Coleman L Blease, a protégé of Benjamin Tillman, the lieutenant governor's uncle. At the request of a New York paper, Tillman released a personal statement through two of his lawyers:

> *I thank you for your courteous and kind telegram in view of the facts that the dispatches sent out from Columbia emanated from the office of* The State *newspaper* [which was not true] *of which Mr. Gonzales was editor. I do not deem it necessary to deny anything that has been sent from that quarter. I can only say that when the truth of the unfortunate affair is known my friends as well as the people of the country will see how thoroughly I was justified in acting as I did. The statements already published in the papers are untrue and at the proper time this I will be prepared to show. Beyond this I do not care to make any further statement.*

Tillman, in his defense, argued that he thought Gonzales was armed, and if not, he should have been. Ironically, Captain James Tillman, nephew of former Governor Benjamin R. Tillman and son of former United States congressman George Tillman, had a history of violence. In January 1895, for example, Captain Tillman exchanged impromptu gunshots with Barnard B. Evans, the younger brother of Governor Martin Gary Evans. Although the Tillman and Evans families are political allies in Edgefield County, there was "bad blood" between Captain Tillman and Barnard Evans. Stories about the altercation varied, but Tillman owed Evans money, and when the two met to settle accounts, shots were exchanged. Each alleged that the other fired first. Regardless of the instigator, both men fired three or four shots each and wounded each other. Evans shot Tillman through the face and hand, and Tillman shot Evans in the shoulder. This incident demonstrates the short-temperedness and pistol-

Above: Benjamin Tillman Monument, statehouse grounds. Asheville Post Card Company, Asheville, North Carolina. *Collection of the author.*

Right: Gonzales Monument obelisk, Senate at Sumter Streets. Erected in 1905, this monument commemorates the courage of N.G. Gonzles. *Photograph by Jacob H. Helsley.*

proneness of both Tillman and Evans and, for the murder of Gonzales, especially of Captain Tillman.

On January 17, schoolchildren, university students and others offered prayers for the editor's recovery. Even the chaplain of the South Carolina Senate, where Tillman had presided before the killing, prayed that Gonzales would survive. The hospital issued bulletins throughout the day.

"A Martyr to the Freedom of the Press"

Four days after the shooting, on January 19, N.G. Gonzales died. On January 20, his brother Ambrose E. Gonzales wrote:

> *The knightly soul of the brave man, loyal friend and devoted bother, whose name has graced these columns since the birth of* The State *twelve years ago, has crossed the river, and the paths his willing feet have trod shall know him no more. But along their ways, from seed he sowed, flowers are blooming and the air he loved to breathe, the air of his native State, is sweet with the incense of his noble words and deeds.*
>
> *To die for his State, even by the loathly hand that struck him down, was sweet to him…He died with his face to God, a gentleman unafraid…and in his name* The State *is pledged anew to the principles for which he gave his life.*

Hundreds of mourners gathered to honor the courageous editor, who is buried in Elmwood Cemetery.

On January 22, a coroner's jury heard testimony concerning the death of Gonzales in the county court room. Present, but not participating, were Solicitor J.W. Thurmond and ex-attorney general G. Duncan Bellinger for the prosecution and C.L. Blease for the defense. The jury heard testimony from the following witnesses: Clerk of Court J. Frost Walker, State Senators G.W. Brown of Darlington County and Thomas Talbird of Beaufort County, James F. Sims, A.G. LaMotte and Dr. A.B. Knowlton, who performed the autopsy.

Walker, for example, testified about the revolvers surrendered by James Tillman. Brown was on the sidewalk at the time but did not see the shooting as he had turned to speak to a female acquaintance. Sims noted that Gonzales grabbed his wound and said, "Shoot again, you coward."

At the time he shot N.G. Gonzales, James H. Tillman of Edgefield District was South Carolina's lieutenant governor. *Courtesy of South Caroliniana Library, University of South Carolina (Photographs 15251 os).*

La Motte was also on the corner that day and remembered the shot shattering the calm of the afternoon. Talbird reported that he, Brown and Lieutenant Governor Tillman left the statehouse together. As they were walking, Tillman was in the middle. He saw Gonzales approaching with his hands in the pockets of his overcoat and heard Tillman say, "I got your message" and the shot.

After listening to the witnesses, the jury deliberated less than five minutes and rendered the following verdict: "We the jury find that the deceased, N.G. Gonzales, came to his death from a gunshot wound at the hand of

James H. Tillman on the fifteenth of January 1903." Members of the coroner's jury, which included many prominent Columbia residents, were: Allen Jones, foreman; Thomas Agnew; G.W. Floyd; Joseph H. Epstin; J.W. Robinson; P.H. Lachicotte; W.J. Keenan; J.W. Gibbes; J.M. Daniels; E.B. Brown; W.D. Love; J.L. Shea; L.T. Levin; and E.B. Clark.

"A TRAVESTY OF JUSTICE"

Tillman had a strong defense team and a well-connected family. At the time, his uncle Benjamin Tillman was the most powerful politician in South Carolina. Early in the proceedings, a few South Carolinians wondered if freedom of the press could withstand a Tillman assault. The Tillman team won the opening skirmish. Despite objections by the prosecutor, the trial

was moved from Columbia, an urban setting and home of the University of South Carolina, to Lexington, a rural area that favored Tillman and his populist politics. Privately, Ben Tillman may have had reservations about James Tillman, but publicly, he campaigned hard for his acquittal.

On June 23, George Johnstone, attorney for the defense, requested a change of venue. He cited pretrial publicity and contended that Tillman could not receive a fair trial in Columbia. His remarks also presaged a defense strategy—an appeal to the "common people"— Ben Tillman's constituents. As Johnstone noted, the defense submitted affidavits

Benjamin Ryan Tillman, a native of Edgefield District, was one of South Carolina's most influential and controversial governors. *Courtesy of South Caroliniana Library, University of South Carolina (Photographs 7500-2).*

from "common people," while the prosecution presented affidavits from the "princes of the earth." The defense prevailed. and the trial was moved.

On September 28, the trial began. During the lengthy trial, the defense fought to exclude witness statements. One victory for the prosecution, as reported by W.W. Ball, came on day three when the court agreed to accept N.G. Gonzales's "dying declaration." On the eighth day, the defense opened with comments—in particular, his editorials—made by the deceased that Tillman took as "threats" that thereby justified the killing. Both defense and prosecution also argued over references to Tillman's famous uncle, Benjamin Tillman. Closing arguments included statements by Solicitor Thurmond and William Elliott Jr. for the prosecution and George Johnstone for the defense. Elliott stated, "It is useless to talk of a defense that a man may shoot another down because he wiggled his thumbs in his pocket." Johnstone commented on a statement that "the rural people of Richland sympathize with Tillman." But there was truth in that comment, and after three weeks of testimony, the Lexington County jury found Tillman not guilty as he had acted in self-defense. The jurors deliberated twenty hours before reaching their decision in October. Reportedly, the verdict was delayed because two jurors held out for conviction.

Press reaction was national in scope. For example, the Chicago *Inter-Ocean* wrote, "As predicted by most observers of the present social conditions of South Carolina, James Tillman was acquitted of the murder…From the Louisville *Courier Journal*, Tillman, the South Carolina murderer, misjudges the American public if he thinks they wish any 'statement' from him. They are familiar with his case…and they know him to be a cowardly assassin." According to the Greenville (NC) *Reflector*, "Jim Tillman goes free and another dark crime goes unpunished." The Augusta (GA) *Tribune* reported, "The verdict of the jury is a travesty of justice." Even in-state papers had similar comments. The Chester (SC) *Lantern* commented, "We are not among those who make the silly pretense of accepting the verdict as just. We believe it should be repudiated by the people of the state."

In honor of Gonzales's life and service to the state, a committee of citizens raised money to erect a memorial. On December 12, 1905, the donors celebrated the life of Gonzales and dedicated the memorial as a gift to the city. The obelisk stands at the corner of Senate and Sumter Streets, across Sumter from the statehouse. The monument—one of

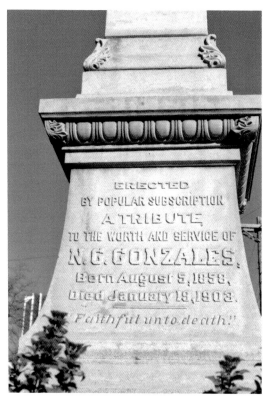

Gonzales Monument inscription. *Photograph by Jacob H. Helsley.*

the few erected to honor a newspaper editor—celebrates Gonzales as a "great editor, an eminent citizen, an honest man…the measure of success is not what we get out of life but what we leave after it."

W.W. Ball was an ardent Tillman critic and the author of *The State That Forgot: South Carolina's Surrender to Democracy*. According to him, Gonzales was one of South Carolina's premier journalists. For example, N.G. Gonzales "never sold the truth to serve the hour." To many, like Ball, he was a martyr to a free press.

James H. Tillman did not have many years to enjoy his freedom. In 1911, he died in Asheville, North Carolina.

Chapter 8

New Century, Old Problems

C olumbia entered the twentieth century poised for growth. Textiles and related manufacturing had brought new economic opportunities and new residents. Commercial development boomed on Main Street with new banks and high-rise buildings. Columbia paved its streets, built a new city hall and jail on Lincoln Street, expanded its boundaries and reaped the economic windfall of a booming military presence. These changes altered the rhythm of life and brought new tears in the fragile fabric of daily life.

DEVILTRY ABROAD

According to the *State*, in January 1908, the Richland County Court of General Sessions had a full docket. Those in jail awaiting trial were: S.F. Byars (murder), Annie Bell Wright (burglary), Mary Wade (burglary), Paul Richardson (grand larceny), George Brennan (grand larceny), Marie Thompson (housebreaking and grand larceny), Nehemiah Johnson (grand larceny), Isaac McKensie (stealing a bicycle), Joe Augustine (attempted assault), Henry McNeal (stealing a bicycle), Dosia E. Clark (murder), Wesley Bishop (assault and battery with intent to kill), Son Williamson (grand larceny), Bill Lovett (murder), R.B.

Statehouse, Columbia, by Walter L. Blanchard, 1913. *Courtesy of South Caroliniana Library, University of South Carolina (Photographs 8351-9).*

Loring (grand larceny), Andrew Couter (grand larceny), Knowlton Davis (murder), Joe Jackson (burglary), Adam Williams (assault and battery with intent to kill), J.B. Walters (grand larceny), Fred Smith (grand larceny), Jack Scott (violation of the dispensary law), Willie Lovley (grand larceny), Dove Garrott (assault and battery with intent to kill), L.H. Felkell (forgery), H.C. Jeanette (forgery), James Moses (carjacking and larceny), John Cannedy Jr. (attempted arson), Moses Goodwin (murder), Tom Cheek (murder), Simpson Cooper (breach of trust), William Washington (assault and battery with intent to kill), John Graham (housebreaking with intent to ravish), Robert Tucker (housebreaking and larceny), Benjamin Leggins (housebreaking and larceny) and John Lawhorn (being held for the county chain gang).

The star turn for the February 17 session was the retrial of Ethel Blair. The state accused Blair of killing her husband, Cullen W. Blair. During the last term, a jury found Blair guilty of manslaughter. Nevertheless, the defense alleged new evidence, and while awaiting a new trial, Blair was out on bond. Another convicted murderer, S.F. Byars, was also awaiting a decision of the South Carolina Supreme Court. A circuit court jury had found Byars guilty of murdering Oliver J. Lanahan with a recommendation for mercy. The solicitor appealed the decision to the Supreme Court.

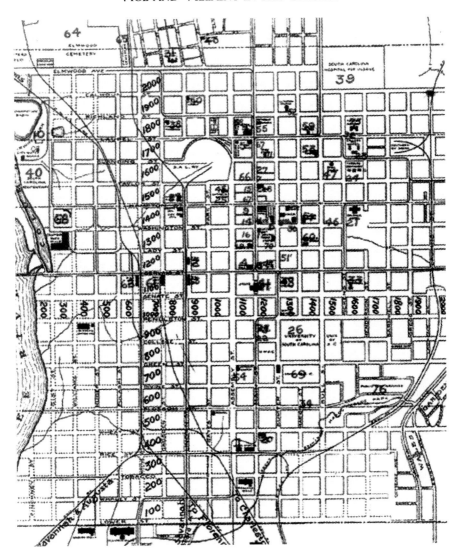

Map of Columbia, 1914. By 1912, Columbia's population exceeded thirty thousand.
Courtesy of the South Carolina Department of Archives and History.

Among the new cases, Knowlton Davis quarreled in a restaurant with another man on Main Street. Afterward, Davis stabbed the man outside the business. Tom Cheek was also accused of killing with a pocketknife. His victim was named George Williams. Cheek and his victim were both inebriated. Perhaps the saddest case involved Dosia E. Clark, charged with the murder of her child.

IN THE LINE OF DUTY

On May 18, 1910, Hilton T. Smith died in Columbia Hospital. While hospital deaths are not unusual, Smith's death was. Smith was the Columbia city jailer. He lived in a cottage in "the yard adjoining the country jail." Jailer Smith frequently performed police duties in the surrounding area—the part of Columbia where the Seaboard Railroad's main line entered Sidney Park from the south. Smith was not the first Columbia law enforcement officer to die in the line of duty, but his death was the first in a number of years. In 1910, the thirty-one-year-old Smith lived on Lincoln Street with his wife and two children.

On that fateful Tuesday, Charity, the wife of John "Bud" Rabb, fled to Smith's cottage for assistance. She told Smith that Rabb had been beating her and had thrown a lamp at her. Finally eluding her tormentor, she ran to Smith and asked him to arrest her husband. Smith then accompanied her to her home on Gadsden Street in Ward 3 and arrested a recalcitrant Rabb. According to the 1910 census, both John and Charity Rabb were thirty-eight years old. They had been married for three years, and her three children lived with them. Rabb was a board planer for a lumber manufacturing company, and Charity Rabb worked as a laundress.

Coming up Taylor Street with Rabb, Smith intended to stop at the call box and summon a patrol wagon for Rabb. Unfortunately, in the

Sidney Park and Park Street, westside next to corner, Blackburn Album, circa 1905. *Courtesy of South Caroliniana Library, University of South Carolina (Photographs 3428 album).*

shadows under the trees, Rabb carefully extricated the officer's gun and shot him.

Rabb fled the scene, but Chief William C. Cathcart of Blaney arrested him and returned him to Columbia police. At that time, Blaney was a flag station on the Seaboard Railroad, twenty miles east of Columbia. After his arrest, Rabb admitted shooting the jailer but blamed "whiskey," saying he was drunk at the time and not responsible for his actions.

The Whole Is Greater Than the Sum of the Parts

Hands down, though, the most gruesome case was the murder of Genevieve "Jennie" Williams on Monday, July 31, 1916. Three days later, on August 2, Williams's mother found her daughter's dismembered body in a trunk in the home of the deceased. At the time of her death, Genevieve Williams lived on Gadsden Street. The murderer had cut Williams into small enough pieces to fit into a medium-sized trunk.

Immediately, officers identified Jesse Murphey as a "person of interest." Murphey and Williams lived together on Gadsden Street, and he disappeared before the body was discovered. Before his disappearance, Murphey worked at a packinghouse on Gervais Street. In their efforts to locate Murphey, officials distributed circulars and broadcast his description. Murphey may be the Jesse Murphy who, in 1910, was a prisoner in the state penitentiary. The 1910 census also lists a twelve-year-old Jennie Williams who lived with her father, David, and sister Sarah on Gadsden Street.

Three years later, on March 10, 1919, a telegram from Pittsburgh informed Columbia police that Murphey was in custody. Clyde S. Edeburn, a detective captain, also noted that Murphey refused to voluntarily return to Columbia. As Columbia police chief J.W. Richardson prepared the necessary paperwork, another telegram arrived with the news that Murphey had confessed to the murder of Genevieve Williams. Richardson traveled to Pittsburgh and returned with Murphey on March 17, 1919. At the time of his arrest, the thirty-four-year-old Murphey worked for a pool room in Pittsburgh.

During questioning in Columbia, Murphey admitted killing Williams but claimed her death was accidental. Around noon on July 31, 1916, Murphey said that he was lying on the bed when Williams attacked him with a fork. He grabbed her and was surprised that he had choked her to death. Murphey further alleged that Williams's body fell into the trunk, which gave him the idea of concealing her body there. Murphey was tried for the murder of Williams and sentenced to be electrocuted. Although the evidence was circumstantial, his admission of guilt placed him at the scene. The jury rejected his pleas of self-defense. His electrocution date was delayed several times, and on August 14, 1920, Governor Archer Cooper commuted Murphey's sentence from death to life imprisonment. The board of pardons and the solicitor supported the commutation of Murphey's sentence.

CORONER AS VICTIM

In 1917, Columbia was rocked by a bizarre murder on an otherwise quiet Sunday. On October 14, around midnight, Jesse N. Helms, a former rural policeman, killed Richland County coroner Jack A. Scott. The two men were close friends, and the news shocked their friends and acquaintances.

The morning after the incident, Magistrate Griffith convened a coroner's jury. Although the testimony revealed little information about a motive, witnesses did provide details about the incident and events leading up to Scott's untimely death. Scott died in Arthurtown, a historic Reconstruction-era neighborhood off Bluff Road.

At the inquest, Dr. W.E. Fulmer testified that "as the mouth was full of sand" and his lip cut, Scott had died face down. Yet, when the sheriff and his deputy found the body, Scott was lying on his back. The first law enforcement representatives to reach the body included the sheriff, his deputy and Magistrate Griffith. Scott's hat and a smoked cigar lay near the body. Another witness, Julius A. Shanklin, arrived at the scene around 12:30 a.m. Shanklin noted that "Scott's body was lying on its back, right arm extended, left arm lying across the body as if it was carefully laid out." In addition, he said, Scott's legs were crossed. Shanklin was the manager of Taylor Dairy. In 1910, according to the census, Shanklin was thirty-five years old and the general manager of a dairy farm. He and his family plus a number of boarders lived on the Taylor Plantation.

William F. Stieglitz, another witness, found a pistol (possibly Scott's) but commented that the barrel was corroded and it did not appear to have been fired. Stieglitz, a native of Germany, was a locksmith. The Stieglitz family lived on Richland Street, Ward 4, Columbia. Stieglitz testified that he did not hear Helms confess to the shooting. Rather, when he asked Helms what had happened, the latter refused to comment.

Mitchell Williams's testimony collaborated Blakely's report. After church, Williams heard a number of shots fired in quick succession. Everyone was excited, so Williams went to investigate. When he reached the dead body, Helms "struck a match and said, 'I killed, but I hated to do it.'" Saying he planned to surrender to the sheriff, Helms asked Williams to watch the body and drove away.

Testimony at the inquest indicated that Helms and Scott spent at least an hour (from 3:00 to 4:00 p.m.) the afternoon before the death drinking together. Tom Blakely, a restaurant owner, stated that the men bought soft drinks and then added liquor from two different pint flasks. According to Blakely, from 3:00 p.m. until 9:00 p.m., the two men were in and out of his restaurant, as they stated, "looking out for violators of the traffic laws." Over time, they became increasingly inebriated and "jolly." Blakely went to church, and when he returned, the two men were "talkative" and "circling around." Blakely continued to his yard and then heard several pistol shots. Helms got Blakely and took him to the body, struck a match and asked Blakely to identify the man. Blakeley replied, "It's Mr. Scott." At which point, as Blakely remembered, Helms said, "I hated to do it, but had to do it." As the nearest telephone was out of order, Helms drove off to contact the sheriff.

Two other observers, E.J. Acree and M.C. Hinson, saw Helms in civilian clothing, flushed and drunk and swearing. Both men worked at the stave factory in Arthurtown and saw Helms at Blakely's establishment.

Another witness, Clara Robertson, on her way home from church, heard the men arguing. According to Robertson, they were "arguing or fussing about a dime, and claiming they ought not to break friendship for 10 cents." Around midnight, she also heard pistol shots.

Dr. W.E. Fulmer, the medical examiner, was the last witness at the inquest. He described the position of the body and the condition of the crime scene. When Fulmer reached the scene, it was almost 1:00 a.m.

[He] *saw the body of Scott lying on its back with legs crossed, one foot resting on the other, right arm was extended and a revolver lay between the right hand and body. To the left of the body was a hat, clots of blood and a cigar stump. An imprint of a nose was visible, the ground looked as if something had lain on it. Dirt or sand was in the mouth, lips were bruised as if they were cut by a fall face downward. A minor bruise was on the left side of the face. A bullet had plowed its way through the man's body, entering on the right side a few inches under the arm and coming out on the left side near the third rib. The bullet had penetrated both lungs and death was almost instantaneous. He could have lived for about two minutes but could not possibly have turned his body over. Another bullet made a flesh wound on the right leg.*

Following Fulmer's testimony, the coroner's jury deliberated and reached its verdict. Members of the coroner's jury were: G.W. Taylor, chairman; C.L. Brazelle; W.S. Brown; J.T. Cheney; J.A. Meetze; A.W. Hamby; J.G. Ehrlich; James McDonald; J.A. Block; W.W. Oliver; W.M. Blackstone; and B.B. Kirkland. The inquest found "that J.A. Scott came to his death by a gunshot wound at the hands of J. Helms." When the verdict was announced, reporters rushed to the Richland County jail to interview Helms. The suspect, nevertheless, upon the advice of his attorney, refused comment.

The accused did not issue a statement until November. Then, preparatory to his bail hearing, he issued an affidavit. Helms stated that Scott arrived at his house in Shandon at 9:30 a.m. on the day of the tragedy. Their day included finding a mechanic to repair Scott's car and traveling to Arthurtown, where Scott warned several motorists who were driving too fast. Helms admitted that the two men visited Blakely's store but denied drinking in excess. According to Helms, Scott then went to Blakely's house as the two men were discussing operating a food stand at the black state fair. When Scott returned, Helms wanted to return to his home as it was dark. But Scott was complaining that "someone had taken $10 from him and he was going to get it before he left." Helms then alleged that Scott accused him of the theft, became belligerent, threatened him, cursed him and "wanted deponent to fight a duel with him." The two men started for the car, but Scott refused to go home without the money. Helms and Scott then argued about the money.

TO SAVE A HOME

In 1919, the Richland County Court of General Sessions had a "record breaking" docket. In two weeks, the court processed over eighty-nine cases. Some defendants entered guilty pleas and others had their day in court. As a result, the *State* reporter noted that thirty more prisoners joined the county chain gang. Despite the full court agenda, attorneys for one defendant

Jefferson Davis Bridge (Gervais Street Bridge) over the Congaree River (U.S. Highway 1) was the site of fateful confrontation in 1919. Asheville Post Card Company, Asheville, North Carolina. *Collection of the author.*

petitioned to add their client's case to the docket. The lawyers argued that the deaths of Arrie B. Lancaster and Newton S. Lorick occurred while the court was in session, so they contended that the court term could be extended to hear the Lancaster case. With the already full docket, the court instead heard already scheduled pending cases with jailed defendants. Consequently, the judge refused the request to add the Lancaster case and instead scheduled it for the September term.

Eugene M. Lancaster, the defendant in the case, was charged with killing his wife, Arrie, and Newton S. Lorick. The story reads like a Hollywood script. Around 4:00 p.m. on May 28, 1919, Eugene M. Lancaster, a motorcycle officer with the Columbia police department, was driving a transport car from Columbia toward West Columbia. As he reached the Gervais Street bridge over the Congaree River, he encountered another vehicle. Newton S. Lorick, a thirty-eight-year-old farmer who lived near Irmo, was driving the other car and Lancaster's wife, Arrie, was in the passenger seat. According to witnesses, Lancaster recognized his wife, left his vehicle and jumped on the running board of Lorick's Buick. When Arrie Lancaster saw her husband, she cried, "My God," and Lorick reached for his revolver. Lancaster then fired eleven shots from two .38-caliber Smith & Wesson revolvers, killing his wife and Lorick. Five bullets hit Mrs. Lancaster, and seven hit Lorick. The driverless car damaged a bridge railing and rolled two hundred feet before stopping near a twenty-five-foot embankment.

Arrie Lancaster was thirty-five years of age and the mother of four children who ranged in age from five to fifteen. Eugene M. Lancaster, a native of Barnwell, moved to Columbia in 1898. During his time in Columbia, he worked for a cotton mill and a lumber company and had been a member of the Columbia police for eleven years. At the time of her death, Arrie and Eugene Lancaster had been married seventeen years and lived on River Drive, where they operated a grocery store.

According to reports, she had left home in the afternoon to attend a movie and was seen around 2:00 p.m. in Lorick's touring car crossing the same bridge traveling toward Lexington. Lancaster, by his admission, was home recovering from a motorcycle accident. He had seen Lorick in the neighborhood, and when his wife left, he followed her. He had fractured his ankle and only recently had been seen walking with crutches. Nevertheless, during the shooting, Lancaster forgot his injury. However, after the shooting, he fell to the ground, and one of the witnesses helped him up, at which point, according to the witness, Lancaster returned to his vehicle and drove to the damaged car and fired more shots. At the police station, he lamented the destruction of his family.

On June 4, 1919, the Richland County Grand Jury returned a "true bill" against Lancaster, charged with killing his wife, and returned another indictment charging him with the murder of Newton S. Lorick. R.H. Howell and James Harman testified before the jury. On June 11, Lancaster's attorneys petitioned for bail, which Solicitor Spigner opposed.

Attorneys C.L. Blease and A.W. Holman represented Lancaster. The attorneys argued that Lancaster should be tried for both deaths at the same time. As Blease stated, "The defendant used two pistols under one impulse as one act and no one could tell which party was hit first or whether the man or woman died first." The judge reviewed the arguments but then refused the motion. So, Lancaster faced two trials—one for the death of his wife and the other for the murder of Lorick. Lancaster was charged with murder and carrying a concealed weapon.

On September 18, the first Lancaster trial began. George Bell Timmerman assisted the solicitor with the prosecution, and Blease and Holman represented Lancaster. At his trial for killing his wife, Lancaster was acquitted. During his trial for the murder of Lorick, Lancaster entered a plea of self-defense. He alleged that when Lorick caught sight of him, he "threw his hand to his side." Lancaster claimed not to remember anything after the first shot, and a doctor testified for the defense that Lancaster was "confused." When questioned, he denied intending to shoot his wife, although five bullets had struck her. Testimony also revealed that during Lancaster's twenty-one days in the hospital for his fractured ankle, several times Lorick brought Arrie Lancaster to visit him. After he returned home, he frequently saw his wife in company with Lorick. Lorick's father lived about seventy-five yards from the Lancaster store.

During the trial, Catherine Nipper, Arrie's mother, testified that she had lived with the Lancasters for several years. While there, she observed arguments and reported that at least once, Lancaster had threatened his wife. The prosecution introduced evidence that Lancaster was aware of his surroundings after the shooting. Magistrate Ollie Mefford of Waverly heard Lancaster say to Deputy Sheriff T. Alex Heise, "My God, Alex," and then ask someone "to watch that damn Lorick crowd and keep them off of me." In response, the defense called Chief J.W. Richardson of the Columbia police. Richardson testified that when he reached the scene of the crime, Lancaster excitedly told him, "This is the scoundrel that ruined my home." Lancaster's attorneys, despite objections by the prosecution, introduced an affidavit from Lancaster's son that his mother was involved with Lorick and that he had seen them together. Given the testimony, the jury returned a verdict of not guilty.

In 1920, Eugene M. Lancaster still lived on River Drive with his four children. The census lists his occupation as grocer.

UNDER THEIR NOSES

In February 1919, Columbia residents heard shocking and surprising news: the courthouse had been robbed. According to officials, someone broke into the vault in the county treasurer's office and stole over $12,000. The crime was an inside job. Janitor Odell Thompson labored several weeks boring into the four-foot-thick walls of the vault. Thompson admitted using stacks of tax books to hide the hole. Thousands of Columbians rushed to the courthouse to visit the crime scene.

Shortly after the theft was discovered, law enforcement arrested Thompson. Thompson admitted his guilt and assisted with the recovery of the stolen money—$12,510. In court, he entered a guilty plea and was convicted of housebreaking and grand larceny. Judge Townsend sentenced a "haggard" Thompson to five years at hard labor.

FATAL VISIT

In November 1919, a visit to Columbia went tragically awry. On October 15, Nick Dulica, a chauffeur from Birmingham, Alabama, left Birmingham to transport a client to Columbia. The client offered Dulica fifteen dollars per day for transporting the man to Columbia. Dulica operated a five-passenger Hudson touring car that he had recently purchased from Reliance Automobile Company. Dulica made the trip successfully, and on October 20, he wrote his family that he was ready to return home. When he did not arrive, his family contacted a detective agency in Birmingham. The agency, in turn, contacted Richardson, Columbia chief of police, for assistance.

According to his family, Nick Dulica was twenty-six years old and stood five feet three inches tall. Dulica had black hair and brown eyes and was wearing a dark suit when he left home.

On November 13, Dulica's body was found in Marlboro County. From the condition of the body, authorities determined that he had not died recently. Dulica died from wounds to his head and torso. His personal effects included his chauffeur's license, a temporary YMCA card (perhaps where he stayed in Columbia), several receipts, nine dollars in cash and a gray Stetson hat with a hole in it. The hole in Dulica's hat suggested that he had been shot or stabbed from the rear. Near the body, authorities discovered a letter addressed to C.D. Cooper with a Birmingham address.

Officials in Columbia requested that their counterparts in Birmingham arrest C.D. Cooper. Unfortunately, Cooper was not found in Birmingham, and the story went cold.

DEADLY SCUFFLE

In May 1919, an altercation broke out at the Dutch Fork Reformatory. Perry Inabinet and Casey Jones argued and fought. The twenty-one-year-old Inabinet, who was serving time for housebreaking, alleged that Jones had attacked him with a knife. Inabinet then knocked down the sixteen-year old Jones and stomped on him. Authorities transported the gravely injured Jones to the state penitentiary, where two physicians operated in a desperate but eventually futile effort to save Jones's life. Unfortunately, the damage to his abdomen from the assault was too severe, and "after intense suffering," Jones died. A magistrate and constable then brought Inabinet to the county jail, where he was charged with murder.

Casey Jones had a well-earned reputation with the police. His photograph was on display in the police barracks. Apparently, Jones gained notoriety by stealing a train in the railroad yards. He coupled a number of boxcars to an engine and was pulling the throttle on the engine headed out of the yard when railroad employees intervened. No one was certain where Jones planned to take the train. Nevertheless, according to the *State*, Jones "became famous the moment he started the train."

On June 3, 1919, Perry Inabinet pled guilty to manslaughter. As a result, he was sentenced to two years of hard labor.

GET OR BE GOTTEN

The year 1919 was a deadly one in Columbia. In June, two men met near the mailbox on the corner of Gervais and Main Streets in front of the Union National Bank and city hall. The men were related by marriage, brothers-in-law. Two young men met, but only one walked away. William J. Staub, according to witnesses, shot C.H. Markey several times. A week later, Markey died of his wounds in Columbia Hospital.

Markey, a native of New York, served in the United States Army. During his army years, he was stationed at Fort Jackson and married Staub's sister Eva. After his enlistment ended, the Markeys decided to settle in Columbia. At the time of his death, Eva and C.H. Markey were the parents of three small children.

Law enforcement arrested Staub for the murder. At his trial, many, including the defendant's sister, Eva Staub Markey, and mother, Mamie Staub, testified for the defense. According to Staub, the men had enjoyed an amicable relationship until fire destroyed their home and furnishings two months earlier. Afterward, Markey seemed to undergo a personality change and became aggressive and abusive. Once, Markey broke into Staub's home, and Staub ran to a neighbor's house for protection. Markey followed Staub and threatened to kill him. To avoid Markey, Staub, who worked on Main Street, changed his route home. Tired of trying to avoid him, Staub sent word to Markey to leave him alone. Staub told officers that "Markey was fixing to ruin his home." So, on that fateful Saturday, when Staub encountered Markey, he expected to be killed. He fired three shots

Main Street looking north from the capitol, by Walter L. Blanchard, 1913. City hall is on the left. *Courtesy of South Caroliniana Library, University of South Carolina (Photographs 8351-7).*

and then dropped the gun. The stray bullet hit a young woman walking on Gervais Street. Officers arrested Staub without incident.

Before Markey died, W.J. Clark, Columbia hospital superintendent, talked with him. Markey knew he was going to die and stated, "I guess Staub thought I would get him before he got me."

Under cross-examination, Staub admitted that Markey did not have a gun or knife. As witnesses for the state testified, Staub began firing around 1:00 p.m. on May 3. The first bullet missed, and Markey kept walking from Staub toward city hall. The second bullet struck Markey, and the third brought him to his knees in front of the office of the Columbia treasurer. As he fell, Markey was clutching his stomach. Although Solicitor Spigner vigorously prosecuted the case and witnesses testified that Markey was unarmed, the jury deliberated only twenty-two minutes before returning with a verdict of "not guilty."

In 1920, the widowed Eva Staub Markey and her three young children lived with her brother, William, and their parents, Joe and Mamie Staub. The Staubs lived on Hampton Street. Joe Staub, born in Switzerland, was employed by the gas company. William Markey and his sister, Eva Markey, worked in a laundry.

THE WRONG PLACE

In March 1920, a ride on a crowded streetcar turned violent. Two men, strangers to one another, jostled on the streetcar. One died, and one faced the electric chair. The incident occurred at the corner of Sumter and Pendleton Streets. Columbia in 1920 was a segregated place. Black and white citizens, for example, sat in separate areas in the courtroom. Legally, public transportation was also segregated. In this case, race made an already difficult situation worse.

Albert Wilson, the accused, was a young African American. Wilson, age twenty-two, had worked nine years for Swift's Oil Company. He lived with his wife and sons in rental housing near Harper's Road in

World War I Memorial, corner of Pendleton and Sumter Streets. *Photograph by Jacob H. Helsley.*

Richland County. His victim—Bryan B. Butler—was a white man. Butler, a three-year army veteran, was twenty-eight years old when he died. He was a house painter by trade. In 1920, Ellen and Bryan Butler boarded with a family on Olympia Avenue.

According to Ellen Butler, widow of the victim, she, Bryan and friend Eva Crouch boarded the streetcar at the city hall stop. It was a Saturday night, and the car was crowded. With no free seats, the Butler party stood at the rear. After the car pulled away from the stop, Ellen Butler heard her husband say, "I'm shot." She was not aware of any conversation or movement around them. Eva Crouch's testimony supported Ellen Butler's. Crouch heard nothing until the gunshot. She saw Butler fall as he was standing near her.

S.L. Meetze, the streetcar conductor, testified that he did not notice when the Butlers, Crouch or Wilson boarded the car. He was at his regular post

North Main Street looking north toward the statehouse, Columbia, by Walter L. Blanchard, March 21, 1913. One of Columbia's streetcars is on the left. *Courtesy of South Caroliniana Library, University of South Carolina (Photographs 8351-3).*

in the rear of the car as it traveled down Sumter Street. Nearby, he heard a gunshot and looked around. Then he saw Wilson with a revolver in his hand. He and other passengers grabbed Wilson, who shouted, "Open that door, or I'll blow out your damn brains." Wilson struggled and tried to escape through a window. Butler fell to the floor. Bystanders carried him to the sidewalk where he expired.

In other testimony, mortician A.S. Dunbar reported that Butler's clothes had a bullet hole and powder burns. Army soldier H.C. Becknell testified that he heard someone near him say, "It's a lie." Then he heard a shot and Butler's last words, "Oh Lord, I am shot." Another witness, Ross Williams, had a different account. He told the court that there were many black and a few white passengers in the rear of the car. He saw Wilson flick cigar ashes on Butler. Butler indignantly cried, "Don't burn my clothes." Wilson replied, "I'll burn your clothes…" and Butler retorted, "I'll knock you through that door." After Wilson dared him to proceed, Butler hit him several times and Becknell heard a gunshot.

Wilson took the stand in his defense. According to his account, around 7:00 p.m., he boarded the crowded car. As the streetcar continued on its route, a sudden turn threw him against Butler. Butler hit him and knocked him into another man, who also hit him. Butler then hit Wilson again. Wilson saw Butler's hand move toward his rear pocket and, in response, pulled his gun. Wilson alleged that someone grabbed his gun, and it fired in the scuffle. He denied smoking a cigar or drinking to excess.

Robert Jenkins testified that Wilson had a cigar, and Butler objected to his smoking. The two men exchanged blows, and the gun went off when the conductor intervened. Others commented on Wilson's good character.

On June 2, 1920, testimony concluded, and the jury convicted Albert Wilson of murder in the first degree. The judge deferred sentencing as Wilson's attorneys planned to request a new trial. That effort failed, and the court set July 8 as the date of Wilson's electrocution. That date passed while the South Carolina Supreme Court considered his appeal.

In a sidebar to this unfortunate situation, Annie Tarlton, a passenger on the streetcar, with her husband, F.S. Tarlton, filed suit against the Columbia Railway, Gas and Electric Company. Tarlton was a textile worker. When the gun fired, Annie Tarlton, believing her life in danger, jumped through a window. She injured her knee in the jump, and her suit sought damages of $10,000. G. Duncan Bellinger and John W. Crews represented the Tarltons in their court action. Annie Tarlton alleged the company was negligent, as the company had not provided "proper and sufficient separate accommodation for white and negro passengers," which was a "violation of both state law and city ordinances."

UNKNOWN BODY

In September 1919, the body of a nude man was found in the Congaree River. Dr. W.A. Boyd examined the body but found no apparent cause of death. Unfortunately, he did not examine the man's lungs to determine if he died before or after he entered the water. Constable A.C. Palmer searched the riverbank and found a wagon track leading to Arthurtown. Consequently, some endorsed a theory that the deceased man was a soldier from Camp Jackson whose clothes were removed to prevent identification. The mystery man was buried in Columbia.

The finding of this body was similar to another body found on the Atlantic Coast Line tracks near James Crossing. That man was similarly stripped and

Sixteenth Company, 156 Depot Brigade, Camp Jackson, S.C., by Rudolph, circa 1918. *Courtesy of South Caroliniana Library, University of South Carolina (Photographs 11197 panorama).*

found in the same vicinity as the mystery man, but his clothing was found under a stump near where the train hit the body.

Law enforcement contacted authorities at the camp to see if anyone matching the mystery man's description was missing.

A PARTNERSHIP GONE SOUR

It was a business deal between work associates. In 1920, John C. Arnette and Frank M. Jeffords worked for the Columbia Compress Company. Arnette was a foreman and Jeffords a manager. At that time, Arnette (age forty-five) and his wife and two young children lived in Eau Claire. The twenty-six-year-old Jeffords, on the other hand, lived with his wife and small daughter on Gadsden Street in Columbia. Both men rented their homes.

At some point in their relationship, the two men decided to become business partners and invested in a service station on Elmwood Avenue. Arnette managed the station, and Jeffords continued with the compress. But the partnership was not successful. Jeffords wanted it dissolved and was willing to buy out Arnette's interest or sell his own. Arnette offered Jeffords $1,000 for Jeffords's interest but wanted $2,000 for his share. Jeffords thought his proposition of fifty-fifty was fair and conferred with local attorney C.T. Graydon, who assured Jeffords that Arnette could not force Jeffords out of the partnership without proper legal proceedings.

On May 9, 1922, at around 11:00 p.m., Arnette died at his service station on the corner of Elmwood Avenue and Main Street. According to his death certificate, coroner Jack Scott ruled his death a homicide. His murderer struck him on the head with an iron bar. The fatal blow fractured his skull.

Aerial view of the capitol, including Main Street Business District. Asheville Post Card Company, Asheville, North Carolina. *Collection of the author.*

Arnette's family buried him in King's Mountain, North Carolina. Arnette, a native of Monticello, had lived in Columbia for only three years.

Six national guardsmen en route home from drill spotted a wrecked vehicle on Kirkland Street near Farrow Road. They found Arnette's body in his car in a ditch near a bridge. When he arrived, the sheriff found bloodstains on the upholstery of the front seat. Examining the scene, Sheriff T. Alex Heise determined that Arnette had died elsewhere and the murderer(s) had placed the body in the car and faked an accident. Thomas Alexander "Cap" Heise (1881–1958) served as sheriff of Richland County from 1921 to 1952.

Later, when Heise learned of a fire at the filling station, he went to the station. There, he found J.C. Parker, a city policeman, a newspaper reporter and Frank M. Jeffords, co-owner of the filling station. Jeffords unlocked the door between the waiting room and the repair shop. In the repair shop, Heise found several pools of blood and evidence that someone had tried to build fires over them, possibly to destroy the evidence.

As the city police were handling the case, Heise accompanied Columbia detectives S.S. Shorter, W.T. Kelly, Bob Broom and Jim Broom to 1529 Hampton Street. That was the address of Ira Harrison, an employee of the service station. There, in Harrison's room, they found him in bed with a "bloody coat hanging on a nail over the bed." The officers awakened Harrison. He admitted the coat was his and that he had "hung it up." At that point, the police arrested him. Officers then arrested Glenn Treece, another station employee. No blood was found on Treece's clothing. At the police station, according to Heise, Harrison and Treece admitted the plot to kill Arnette and implicated Frank M. Jeffords.

Sheriff Alex Heise arrested Jeffords and charged him with murder. The prosecution alleged that Jeffords and his accomplices, Harrison and Treece, had killed Arnette in order to collect the payout from Arnette's insurance policy. Arnette had named Jeffords as his beneficiary.

The grand jury indicted Jeffords, Harrison and Treece in the murder of Arnette. On May 11, at their arraignment, Solicitor A. Fletcher Spigner read the indictment charging them with the murder of Arnette. When asked, the three men entered pleas of "not guilty." For the arraignment, Ira Harrison's attorney, John Hughes Cooper, acted as counsel for the three men. Glenn Treece's attorney, E. Beverly Herbert, was not in court for the arraignment. Frank M. Jeffords informed the judge that he did not have an attorney. At that time, the court appointed James H. Hammond to represent Jeffords and, at Hammond's request, named John F. Quinn to assist Hammond with the defense. As the county jail was overcrowded, the accused were housed in the state penitentiary until their trial. Though in the regular cellblock, the men were housed in separate and not contiguous cells. When visited at the penitentiary, reporters noted that Treece appeared the least concerned, Jeffords was "morose" and Harrison nervously voluble.

At the time of his arraignment, Jeffords, a Columbia native, was a thirteen-year employee of the Columbia Compress Company. Arnette, as noted above, had also worked at the Columbia Compress as a foreman. About six months before the tragedy, the two men became partners in the service station at the corner of Elmwood Avenue and Main Street.

Harrison, another one of the defendants, was a native of Hampton County, South Carolina. To officers, he admitted striking Arnette. The twenty-one-year-old Harrison had lived in Columbia most of his life and served in the United States Navy. His enlistment ended in December, and when he returned to Columbia, he began working at the filling station. Harrison had known Treece and Jeffords about four years. According to court records, Harrison was the only one of the three with a criminal record. Prior to his naval enlistment, a Lexington court sent him to the penitentiary to serve a six-month sentence. As he was a juvenile at the time, he was released on a writ of habeas corpus.

The third defendant, Glenn Treece, was twenty-two years old at the time of the arraignment. Born in Asheville, North Carolina, he had lived in Columbia four years. Another navy veteran, Treece also worked at the filling station.

The trial was scheduled to open on May 16. At the trial, Jeffords's attorney asked to have the Jeffords case tried separately, but the judge ruled that the three had been indicted together and so would be tried together. The prosecution took three days to present its case against the accused. They called twenty-three witnesses to shore up the alleged confessions of the accused. According to Heise and other officers, the three defendants had admitted their involvement in a plot to kill Arnette in order for Jeffords to collect on his $4,000 life insurance policy.

U.S. Post Office (now SC Supreme Court Building), Gervais Street. A "Colourpicture" Publication, Boston, Massachusetts. *Collection of the author.*

Federal Land Bank (AgFirst Building). *Photograph by Jacob H. Helsley.*

On May 20, the jury convicted the three men of murder, but Treece's conviction included a recommendation for mercy. The verdict was read at 6:20 p.m. With "the crowded court room held in awesome silence," the judge sentenced Jeffords and Harrison to death in the electric chair and Treece to life imprisonment. On May 21, the three convicted men entered the state penitentiary. Jeffords and Harrison spent their first day in the death house awaiting execution, while Treece began serving his sentence. Also in the death house were three men convicted of killing a Columbia bus driver.

Jeffords denied any involvement with the death of Arnette and stated that "at the time of the murder he did not know that the business insurance policy" was in effect, as there was an unpaid premium.

Attorneys for both Jeffords and Harrison appealed the decision of the lower court. In the appeal of Jeffords's conviction, his attorney argued that Judge Townsend had erred in his charge to the jury about the conspiracy. Harrison's attorney also appealed based upon the judge's charge of "implied malice." Unfortunately for them, the justices upheld the convictions and the actions of Judge Townsend. The South Carolina Supreme Court sent the cases back to the Richland County Court of General Sessions so that the court could set the date for their electrocution. During the appeal process, Treece, whose conviction carried a recommendation for mercy, was already in the penitentiary serving his life sentence.

After that setback, Jeffords then appealed to the United States Supreme Court. Jesse H. Adams of Washington represented Jeffords before the Supreme Court. Adams argued that Jeffords had not had "a fair and impartial trial" as prescribed by the United States Constitution. Although Adams doubted the court would hear the case, he refused to pass up this final opportunity to save his client. After considering the request, Chief Justice William Howard Taft ruled that the Jeffords case involved no federal issues. Consequently, as the State noted, "All that remains for Frank M. Jeffords to do is to die." With all avenues of appeal exhausted, the court set December 22 as Jeffords's execution date.

With this date rapidly approaching, Jeffords's last hope was Governor Wilson Godfrey Harvey. Lieutenant Governor Harvey became governor of South Carolina when Governor Robert Archer Cooper (1874–1953) resigned May 20, 1922, to become a member of the Federal Farm Loan Board. Harvey was a native of Charleston.

On behalf of his client, attorney L.G. Southard appealed to the governor to have Jeffords's sentence commuted. In addition, Jeffords personally wrote Governor Harvey requesting clemency:

Being advised by my attorney that all legal steps have been exhausted in my case and being under sentence of electrocution between the hours of 10 am and 2 pm on December 22, 1922, I have the honor to petition your excellency to commute the sentence from death to another form of punishment.

In considering my petition I beg to call to your attention that I was tried when public sentiment was at white heat against me; so apprehensive was the sheriff of Richland county for my safety before trial I was lodged in the state penitentiary for safekeeping. It was charged that the crime was committed on May 9, 1922. The coroner's jury reported on May 10, I was indicted on May 11 and date for trial set that date. I was placed on trial three days thereafter so apprehensive was the sheriff for my safety and for fear that I would be lynched, I was taken by a circuitous route to and from the court house to the penitentiary. The judge had every one searched except court officials. I asked to be tried separately and apart from Harrison and Treece, but this was denied me. The testimony relied upon by the state for my conviction came from the mouths of Treece and Harrison. They charged that all three of us had formed a conspiracy to kill Mr. Arnette. This I denied and do now deny. The record shows that Harrison admitted hitting Mr. Arnette the first lick, and he says that he does not know whether or not that lick killed him. Treece was recommended to life and is now serving a life sentence.

I have an old mother, 70 years of age, and I feel that my electrocution will kill her. I have three sisters and brothers; I have a dear wife and small child, a little girl six years of age. I beg of you that for their sake you permit me to live, and commute this sentence.

If there are any facts about my case that your excellency desires to know or if you desire a hearing on this matter, I ask you permit L.C. Southard of Spartanburg, who is my attorney, appear before your excellency and explain anything in my case which you might wish to know.

Finally, I feel that being permitted to live I would be a living example to all young men who are drifting into wrong paths and ways and that thus I would be able to cause them to stop and think.

His mother, sister and a number of others wrote the governor supporting Jeffords's clemency petition. A few individuals also wrote opposing clemency. Southard asked Graydon to corroborate Jeffords's account that the men had met on the day of the murder. The key point was the time of the Jeffords/Graydon conversation. Jeffords said he saw the attorney the evening of the murder and was relieved by what he heard. Southard thought this evidence eliminated the possibility of premeditation in Arnette's death. Yet, while Graydon acknowledged that Jeffords had visited him on the day of the murder, he stated that the visit was in the afternoon. Consequently, he did not think his recollection would benefit Jeffords's clemency appeal. Jeffords also asserted that, while he was aware of the insurance policy, he did not know it was still in effect. He thought the policy was not in effect because payment was due.

In reply, Governor Harvey wrote a personal letter to Jeffords. According to the letter, the contents of which were released to the press, Harvey refused to intervene and save Jeffords from electrocution. Harvey wrote, "Interference by me solely on the grounds of kindness, sympathy and good will, would be to flaunt the duly provided system of trial provided by law." The governor also noted "how sorry" he was for Jeffords and that he sympathized with those who loved Jeffords and wished "'some real justification warranted me in being of help to you."

On December 22, 1922, a few days before Christmas, Jeffords was taken from his cell to the death house. In an interview on December 21, Jeffords said, "I am ready to meet my God. Everything is right with me." When asked if he wanted to make a statement, he declined and also refused to comment on Harrison, citing the old adage that if one cannot say something good about someone, one says nothing. Nevertheless, the condemned man thanked

Electric chair at the South Carolina Penitentiary. With grim humor, inmates and others referred to South Carolina's electric chair as "Old Sparky." *Records of the Department of Corrections, Courtesy of the South Carolina Department of Archives and History.*

prison officials for their care. Many tried to visit Jeffords during his last day, but only family members, such as his two brothers, and clergy were admitted. The two clergymen who visited Jeffords were the Reverend P.D. Brown, pastor of Ebenezer Lutheran Church, Richland Street, and the Reverend Mr. H.A. McCullough, pastor of St. Paul's Lutheran Church, Bull Street.

While Jeffords was eating his last dinner, Ira Harrison, his convicted co-conspirator was, as the *State* noted, "in his apparent state of coma." The word "apparent" indicated the reporter's skepticism about Harrison's medical condition. Harrison had been in a "coma" since his resentencing but reportedly was improving. Harrison, although sentenced at the same time as Jeffords, was not facing imminent death. His execution was stayed by an appeal to the Supreme Court and a reprieve by the governor. As Jeffords had noted in his letter to the governor, Harrison's confession was the only direct evidence linking Jeffords to the crime. The other evidence was primarily circumstantial.

Jeffords died in the electric chair on December 22. Prior to his electrocution, Captain Roberts read the death sentence and asked Jeffords if there was anything he could do for him. Jeffords asked that the captain ensure that his suitcase, belongings and Bible were returned with his body to his family. Also, he asked Roberts to donate his fruit to "the boys" and gave the captain two letters for his brothers. At that point, the penitentiary superintendent called the governor to see he had any comment. For example, the governor could have ordered a temporary reprieve. Governor Harvey had nothing to say.

Jeffords never admitted guilt but issued a warning—"I hope my death will be an example to all those in here and those on the outside." As his last words, Jeffords repeated Psalm 23 as a prayer. As he entered the death chamber, he looked around the room and, as he was seated in the chair, addressed the crowd of thirty-five or forty who watched the electrocution. "Good morning, gentlemen." At 10:22 a.m., Dr. R.T. Jennings, the prison doctor, pronounced him dead. During his time in prison, two ministers often visited with Jeffords. Following his death, Reverend McCullough issued a statement for himself and Reverend Brown. As a result of their time with him and sharing Christian materials, Jeffords was united with the Lutheran church by confirmation and received the Lord's Supper before his death. Later that morning, the two ministers conducted Jeffords's funeral at Elmwood Cemetery, and a sad saga ended.

PROHIBITION, OR "LIQUOR, LIQUOR, EVERYWHERE"

As an outgrowth of the Progressive Movement, many South Carolinians favored prohibition. In 1914, according to one letter to the editor, the liquor situation in Columbia was complicated. While the state of South Carolina legally permitted liquor sales, the city of Columbia had a law against the illegal sale of liquor. In 1917, C.P. Hodges complained in a letter to the editor, "We have voted for it and worked for it and won it, and still we have liquor, liquor, everywhere." According to Hodges, there were "a motley crew of ragged men, women and children at every depot… waiting for the train…and then see them going every direction with their gallon to their blind tiger dens."

In 1919, the United States went dry. Ratification of the Eighteenth Amendment prohibited the manufacture and sale of alcoholic beverages in the United States. The news of the ban prompted at least one Columbia druggist to work at augmenting his supply. Willie Bell offered to furnish the druggist with gallons of whiskey at a discount price. Initially, Bell offered the druggist three gallons of "real liquor" for the bargain rate of thirty-six dollars.

Bell and the prospective buyer traveled toward Lady Street. Bell stopped the car and entered a house. He returned shortly, alleging that the seller was reluctant to be seen and wanted the money in advance.

Hotel Jerome. *Courtesy of South Caroliniana Library, University of South Carolina (Postcards rich co 234).*

The druggist paid Bell, but rather than deliver the promised whiskey, Bell disappeared with the cash.

The police arrested Bell. Tried and found guilty, he was sentenced to two years of hard labor.

NO HANDS TIED

On May 23, 1922, Mayor Coleman sent a letter to F.S. Strickland, Columbia chief of police. The mayor assured Strickland that he and the city council would support his efforts to enforce the law. Promising a "free hand in law enforcement," Coleman wrote, "Your hands will not be tied." Coleman's letter detailed the law enforcement issues facing Columbia. Not only were there houses of prostitution, despite the great crackdown of 1917, but call girls frequented Columbia hotels, and street walkers plied their trade on Columbia's broad avenues. In addition, gambling houses were plentiful and pool halls were open to minors. On top of this litany of urban crime, well into the Prohibition era, the liquor business flourished.

Coleman also praised the cleanliness of the city jail and the discipline of Columbia's policemen—in his opinion, "a big improvement over what it formerly was." He expressly asked that Strickland close the houses of prostitution. He suggested that even if there were insufficient evidence to convict, merely arresting suspected prostitutes and streetwalkers would send the message that Columbia was not a profitable place to operate. For a man who professed his willingness to give Strickland "a free reign," his letter was peppered with advice for Strickland. Not only did he have an answer to the prostitution issues, but he also suggested having patrolmen on their beat routinely visit pool halls. As they walked through, they could keep their eyes open for underage visitors.

Chapter 9

"A Devil of a Place"

The year was 1933. South Carolinians were in the depths of the Great Depression. In November 1932, the nation had elected Franklin Delano Roosevelt as president. After his inauguration in 1933, during his first "hundred days" in office, he and Congress initiated sweeping programs to address unemployment and economic recovery. Yet as the year drew to a close, there were still millions of unemployed, and workers of all ages scrambled for jobs.

Christmas Eve, normally a happy family time, took a dark turn. That Saturday, a fifteen-year-old disappeared from the steps of the statehouse. According to his mother, a man had called the previous day and offered the young man a job distributing gifts to poor children. Even though it was his birthday, Hubbard Harry Harris Jr. eagerly accepted the offer of forty cents per hour for up to six hours. Harris, known as "Hub" or "Son," was an eighth grader at Hand Junior High School in Shandon. His father, Hubbard H. Harris, was general superintendent and vice-president of Home Store, Inc., a grocery chain. Hubbard's parents, Hubbard H. Harris Sr. and Martha M., were natives of Georgia. They lived on Pinewood Street with their two children, Hubbard Jr. and Jane.

Hubbard and a friend drove to the 700 block of Main, where he left his car. They reported to the thrift store at 716 South Main, where they met a middle-aged bespectacled man who only wanted to employ Hubbard. Hubbard Harris Jr. was to make distributions for a charity in the southwestern part of Columbia. His friend then watched him leave in a 1928 or 1929 model Whippet automobile painted tan or grey.

Hand Middle School, Wheat Street, where Hubbard was a student in 1933. *Photograph by Terry L. Helsley.*

Hubbard had another job scheduled for the afternoon. At 3:00 p.m., he had promised to mow a neighbor's yard. So when he did not return home in time for his work, his parents reported him missing. According to the news report published on Christmas Day, state and local officials requested federal assistance. Dwight Brantley, agent in charge of the Charlotte office of the Federal Bureau of Investigation, shared his expertise with law enforcement. According to the *State* newspaper, the Harris case was the "first kidnapping case as far as is known in the history of the State." A "liberal" reward was offered for information. According to the newspaper, Hubbard was fifteen years old, had sandy hair and hazel eyes and weighed 115 pounds. At the time of his disappearance, the bareheaded Hubbard wore a blue sweater, blue shirt, grey knickerbockers and socks and black shoes.

Officers involved in investigating the case were Sheriff Thomas A. "Alex" Heise, Columbia Police Chief William H. Rawlinson, Officers Shull L. Shorter and Robert F. Broome and L.O. Carver and F.L. McGaraghy, agents from the Charlotte office of the Federal Bureau of Investigation. Sheriff Heise called the abduction and murder of Hubbard "the worst in the history of Richland County."

On Monday, by chance, three men found Harris's body in an abandoned farmhouse near a swamp eleven miles from Columbia. The Quit Miller house stood thirty yards off Lovers' Lane, about two miles from the point where this road turns off to the right from Bluff Road. Hubbard's body was found in a front room covered by waste cotton and pieces of an old mattress.

On Monday night, authorities arrested Robert H. Wiles, an automobile mechanic who lived on the Winnsboro Road. According to the investigators, several clues led them to Wiles. First, he matched the description given by witnesses who had seen the abduction. Second, authorities located the vehicle that Hubbard had entered. According to investigators, Wiles had borrowed the automobile from Will Kennedy, who lived on Elmwood Avenue. After Hubbard's disappearance, Wiles had left the car behind the Western Union Telegraph Company.

Officers questioned Wiles several times. Eventually, the sad story emerged. Wiles single-handedly hatched a plan to kidnap a young man from a well-to-do family and hold him for ransom. Two weeks earlier, he visited the Harris neighborhood, considered several other young men and finally settled on Hubbard Harris. Without arousing suspicion, Wiles briefly spoke with the

A bungalow on Pinewood Street. In 1933, the Hubbard family lived on Pinewood Street. *Photograph by Terry L. Helsley.*

young man while he was playing football with a friend in his yard. Later, Hubbard told his mother about talking with a "nice" but poorly dressed man.

On December 23, Wiles called the Harris house from the pay phone at a local hotel and discussed a possible job with Hubbard's mother. She checked with her son and confirmed the appointment for the twenty-fourth. Saturday morning, Hubbard and a friend drove to a rendezvous point and parked his car. They met Wiles, who said he only wanted Hubbard. His friend watched as Wiles drove away with Hubbard Harris. Wiles planned to lure Hubbard from home, hide him at the home of a friend and demand a $1,000 ransom from Hubbard's father. Once the senior Harris had delivered the ransom to Wiles near Caughman's pond, Wiles expected to release the boy.

Unfortunately for all, that is not how events unfolded. Wiles picked up Hubbard, drove down Bluff Road, turned right below Doc Roger's store onto an unpaved road and stopped at the Quit Miller place. According to Wiles, he had "planted 100 acres of oats there when his [Quit's] son George Miller died." At the Miller place, Wiles discovered that the house was abandoned and his acquaintance gone. Without anyone to guard young Harris, Wiles led him through the house and out to the barn. There, apparently, Hubbard realized that there was no job and said to Wiles, "This is a devil of a place." According to Wiles, he assured him, "We'd get used to it." He then assigned Hubbard to try and get water from a pump. When Hubbard leaned over to prime the pump, Wiles struck him several times with a heavy railroad angle iron. He then dragged the body to the empty house and tried to hide it in one of the front rooms. Wiles also stole money from the young man and took his wristwatch. Wiles left the watch for safekeeping with Clayton Abernathy, who had a poolroom at the corner of Gervais and Heidt Streets. When he learned the situation, Abernathy turned the watch over to the police.

While Wiles admitted the crime, saying, "I committed the crime and I'll go before the court and ask for mercy," the details he supplied varied and his motive remained unclear. Ransom was the confessed motive, but investigators found no evidence that Wiles needed food, lodging or money. In fact, Wiles told investigators that he was not desperate for money. He had a place to live and had adequate food on hand. Wiles raised chickens and ducks and had recently butchered a hog. Also, he had recently worked as a mechanic. Nevertheless, Wiles noted, "Money will save [keep]. You can use it any time." In 1930, Robert Wiles lived with his wife at a campground in Richland County.

As a gesture of respect, Sol Kohn, president of the Columbia Merchants' Association, announced that many Columbia businesses would close during

Hubbard's funeral. Jane Perry, president of the Hand Junior High School student body, also urged all the students to meet at the school before the service and attend the funeral as a group.

On Thursday, December 28, the Hubbard family buried their son, a "popular and promising boy." Reverend F. Ray Riddle of Shandon Presbyterian Church, assisted by Reverend J.W. Joyner, pastor of Rose Hill Presbyterian Church, conducted the funeral. For the recessional, the church organist played "Abide with Me" and "Jesus Savior of My Soul." Hundreds attended to show their sympathy and support for the family. The active pallbearers were: C.G. Castles, J.L. Gibbons, J.H. Phinney, W.P. Newton, J.A. Barden and George T.

Reverend F. Ray Riddle conducted Hubbard's funeral in Shandon Presbyterian Church, on Wilmot Street. *Photograph by Terry L. Helsley.*

McGregor. Honorary pallbearers included Hubbard's friends; the session; the board of deacons and the members of Hubbard's Sunday school class at Shandon Presbyterian Church. Hubbard H. Harris Jr. was buried at Elmwood Cemetery.

Wiles had his day in court; the jury found him guilty of murder, and H.F. Rice sentenced him to death. On February 21, 1934, Robert H. Wiles entered the South Carolina Penitentiary. Records of the penitentiary indicate that Wiles, a native of Richland County, was literate, forty-nine years old, 5 feet 6¼ inches tall and weighed 126 pounds. Wiles did not appeal his conviction, and on March 12, 1934, he died in the state's electric chair. J.W. McCormick, a Columbia mortician, handed his funeral arrangements. And so the curtain fell on one unusually dark chapter in Columbia's long history. But evil has no end, and other atrocities have followed.

DEATH BY SPILLED MILK

Unfortunately, the abduction and murder of Hubbard Harris was not the only senseless crime of the 1930s. In March 1936, spilled milk triggered a violent confrontation that left a young restaurant employee dead. On March 18, a foursome—Ernest Gates, Myrtle Fink, Lillian Williams and T.K. Kelly Jr.—pulled into the Pig Trail Inn around 10:00 p.m. They ordered sandwiches and milk. A carhop named Seegars (possibly Frank W. Seegars Jr.) took their order and delivered the food. According to Seegars and other witnesses, the waiter warned Gates that the car door was ajar and that the food would spill if the door were closed. Gates closed the door, and the milk spilled. He yelled for a towel, and Seegars, who was otherwise occupied, asked Robert E. Bouknight, who normally worked in the back, to take a towel to the customer.

Bouknight wiped off the car, and as he was removing the tray, Gates yelled, "Take that damned tray off the car." When Bouknight replied that he was removing the tray, a belligerent Gates left the car, approached Bouknight and told him "not to get smart." Gates hit the seventeen-year old, who pushed him away. At that point, Gates opened a knife and stabbed the unarmed Bouknight. He then tried to find Seegars and also threatened

Strait's Cabin Camp, U.S. 1, two miles north of the statehouse. After killing Bouknight over a spilled glass of milk, Gates and Kelly fled to a cabin camp on the outskirts of Columbia. *Courtesy of the South Caroliniana Library, University of South Carolina (Postcards rich co 544).*

another employee named Clarence Seawell. In 1930, Seawell lived with his family on Gadsden Street. At that time, his father, Coy P. Seawell, was an insurance agent.

The horrified employees notified their manager, T.S. Gunnells, who rushed to the scene, dispatched an employee to drive Bouknight to the Baptist Hospital and contacted the police. Meanwhile, Gates and his friends drove away. In 1930, Bouknight lived with his parents and siblings on Park Street. His father, Joe T. Bouknight, was an automobile mechanic.

On March 19, at the urging of Gates and Kelly, Williams reported the car stolen. Chief of Police W.H. Rawlinson challenged her story and sent Detective W.T. Scott to bring her in for questioning. When interviewed later, Williams stated that the two men—Gates and Kelly—had been drinking. She admitted helping them back into the car. Rather than driving directly to her home (1227½ Taylor Street), the foursome drove out Main Street to Sesquicentennial State Park and returned to Columbia by Highway 1. At Gates's suggestion, they parked the car in the 1700 block of Bull Street and walked four blocks to the Taylor address. There, to avoid detection, they entered through the building's rear door. When Gates and Kelly learned that the police were involved, they left to spend the night at a tourist camp near the city limits. With Williams's assistance, the police located and

Columbia Township Auditorium, Elmwood Avenue, the site of the inquest into the death of Robert E. Bouknight. Asheville Post Card Company, Asheville, North Carolina. *Collection of the author.*

arrested Gates and Kelly. On March 20, the fracas took an ugly turn when Bouknight died.

On March 23, according to the *State* newspaper, the coroner held an inquest into the death of Robert Bouknight in the basement of Township Auditorium. Over four hundred attended the inquest. Members of the coroner's jury were M.C. Howard, Mr. Fallaw, Charles L. Kelly, G.W. Jenkins, J.L. Hinson and J.C. Parks. The inquest jury found Gates at fault for the death of Bouknight.

Chapter 10
Hands in the Cookie Jar

In 1942–43, the South Carolina legislature launched a major investigation of the state's penal system. This was not the first, nor the last, investigation of the penal system. For example, the state ordered investigations in 1868, 1869 and 1900. In January 1912, Governor Coleman Blease sent a message to the South Carolina legislature about the state penitentiary. The flamboyant Blease rose to political power as the spokesman for South Carolina's millworkers. In his message (no. 18), Blease asked the legislature to develop a tuberculosis care facility for prison inmates at the Lexington farm and provide fresh food and ensure outside exercise. In addition, he proposed that inmates be used as labor for constructing the new mental health facility. According to Blease, the state was paying laborers one dollar per day, while prison officials were leasing prison labor for fifty-seven and a half cents per day, and the state provided room, board, clothing and medical care. Blease also opposed whipping and other physical punishment for the inmates. In addition, he thought enforced labor in the prison's hosiery mill increased the inmates' likelihood of developing tuberculosis.

Letters from physicians and health officials supported the governor's position. For example, in a letter dated July 19, 1911, W.M. Lester, a member of the South Carolina Board of Health, stated that, in his opinion, "The two principal sources of danger to health at the penitentiary are the female prison building and the hosiery mill." Apparently, there was support for improving conditions at the women's prison. Nevertheless, the hosiery mill remained a source of contention. As Lester noted, research

Nighttime scene on Main Street looking toward the Capitol, Columbia, S.C. Asheville Post Card Company, Asheville, North Carolina. *Collection of the author.*

showed that "close work in cotton or other textile factories, knife grinding, stonecutting, etc, are notoriously prone to favor the development of pulmonary troubles"—for example, pneumonia, influenza, tuberculosis and similar contagious illnesses.

Blease was not successful in closing the hosiery mill as a health threat in 1912, even though, according to statistics compiled by Frederick Hoffman, "the recorded mortality of woolen mill workers includes 106 deaths, of which 26 or 24.5 percent were from consumption." An earlier effort in 1899 was similarly unsuccessful. Despite Blease's efforts and expert opinions, the South Carolina Senate referred the governor's message to the committee on penitentiary.

PRISONS: THEFT AND SEX

In 1940, William A. Huey was superintendent of the Girls' Industrial School in Columbia. According to the census, Huey and his family had relocated to Columbia from Atlanta and lived on Henderson Street. According to his obituary, William A. Huey was a native of Union, South Carolina, a World War I veteran and an ordained Baptist minister. During his years in the ministry, Huey served as pastor of the First Baptist Church, Richmond, Virginia; Citadel Square Baptist Church, Charleston; Belle View Baptist Church in Memphis, Tennessee; and First Baptist Church, Atlanta. Huey died in 1975 in Columbia. His residence was on Gervais Street. His obituary published in the *State* included the following statement: "For several years he served with the National Youth Administration headquartered in Columbia. He returned to his ministerial work in 1943." His obituary did not mention the investigation.

In 1942, rumors were widespread alleging improprieties at the state penal institutions. In response, the South Carolina legislature, as recorded in "Evidence and Testimony, with Exhibits and Affidavits taken at Hearing Before Committee investigating Penal Institutions of South Carolina," created a committee to investigate the following:

> *Treatment accorded prisoners confined in the Penitentiary…*
> *Leaves of absence granted without authority…*
> *Sale of commodities, livestock…produced on the State Farm…*
> *Purchases of supplies to be used by Penitentiary…*
> [and] *other questionable transactions.*

Three sudden and unexpected resignations set tongues wagging. In short order, the superintendent of the Penitentiary (John M. Glenn), captain of the guard and superintendent of the Women's Prison resigned their positions.

THE GIRLS INDUSTRIAL SCHOOL

The investigation of W.A. Huey, superintendent of the Girls Industrial School, included oral interviews and written transcripts. Allegations suggested that Huey was "familiar" with some of the young women in his care, taking them riding and granting them other privileges. One of the employees interviewed was Hugh Brown, who resigned, effective the first of April or "as soon after as I can be relieved." Brown's testimony included interesting sidelights on the operation of the Girls Industrial School: "People come here for all kind of purposes. I had a soldier come to my place the other day at five o'clock & wanted to know if I had a place to sleep." Another time, four soldiers arrived in a cab and set the woods on fire. Then they "complained when the female inmates didn't arrive to extinguish the blaze." Brown averred that he considered the current administration too lenient and noted that "25 or 30 girls had run away when I came, and they are still out." At one time, fifteen or sixteen young women ran away, and Brown had to get them back. The runaways included Peggy Drucker, Emma Gray Dority, Frances Ellis and Rowdena Smith (married).

For the investigators, Peggy Drucker was a person of interest. Drucker's parents, Nita Carter and George A. Drucker Jr., were separated, so Drucker had lived in an orphanage before she entered the school for girls.

According to other testimony, Aleitha Shealey had lived in a house of prostitution. Eva Hurt was the madam of the house at 1019 College Street, a few blocks from the market on Assembly Street.

THE WOMEN'S PENITENTIARY

Investigators were collecting affidavits that women from the penitentiary visited local hotels for sexual purposes. In one affidavit, a bellhop from the Wade Hampton Hotel reported seeing an acquaintance—Travis Goodman (Mrs. Redin Pittman)—at the hotel. She was registered as "Mary Saunders," an alias, and was serving a life sentence for killing a doctor in Sumter.

Several resigned as a result of the report: Colonel John Glenn, superintendent of the Penitentiary; Captain of the Guard L.H. Rourk and Captain Cantey. According to the report, these men had ordered women out of the Women's Penitentiary for "bad purposes."

On January 6, 1942, Travis Goodman Pittman filed an affidavit as part of the investigation. She stated that Captain Rourk twice transported her from the women's to the men's penitentiary to "make some curtains." On the second trip, he told her to be ready at 9:00 a.m. the next morning. He sent a driver to pick her up, and that was the first time she "was ever intimate with him…in one of the upstairs bedrooms." After that initial visit, Pittman visited Glenn several times a week for the same reason during the months of November, December and January. Either in January or February, Glenn's chauffeur Harry Anderson picked her up, but instead of taking her to the penitentiary, he drove to the governor's office. There, Glenn joined her and, citing new developments in her case that required confidential discussion, took her to the Wade Hampton Hotel. At the hotel, Pittman and Glenn again had relations. There were other visits to the Wade Hampton and Marmac Hotels. Glenn arranged leaves for her so that she could spend the time with him. At times, he promised to arrange for her release from prison. At one time, she feared she was pregnant, and Cantey arranged medication causing her to have a miscarriage. According to Pittman, the last she saw Glenn was December 22, 1941.

Statehouse with Mexican War Monument. Asheville Post Card Company, Asheville, North Carolina. *Collection of the author.*

STATE PENITENTIARY

According to an affidavit filed by W.H. Munn, his father was serving a three-year term for manslaughter in the state penitentiary. Munn paid $400, and his father was released the next day.

Grover C. Rush, a penitentiary employee, also testified on September 5, 1941, that on September 30, 1940, he paid Colonel John M. Glenn, superintendent of the State Penitentiary, $200. At the time, he was serving five years for rape. After the payment and serving less than two years of his sentence, the superintendent gave him a leave of absence for the remainder of his term. Also submitted in evidence was a receipt for $200 signed by Grover C. Rush, yardman at the state penitentiary. According to the receipt, Groce Williams paid Rush $200 for the release of his son, James Williams. On September 26, 1940, James Williams, a prisoner from Kershaw County, was authorized a leave of absence from the state penitentiary.

In addition to evidence of female prisoners making illicit visits to the Wade Hampton Hotel and bribes being paid for early release of penitentiary inmates, other evidence suggested misuse of penitentiary property and

State penitentiary, circa 1909. Between 1868 and 1943, the South Carolina legislature launched several investigations into the operations of the penitentiary. *Courtesy of South Caroliniana Library, University of South Carolina (Photographs 11622-10).*

improper disposition of produce and livestock produced by prison farms. For example, there were revised receipts for the sale of livestock with instructions to "just destroy other letter and one we made out the afternoon I saw you" and interesting correspondence between Glenn and Captain W.A. Rush of Boykin. One telling phrase read as follows: "I guess you had better tell Mack to let every thing [*sic*] stay at the farm for some one [*sic*] might not understand as well as I do and I wouldn't do any thing [*sic*] that wasn't right for all the dogs and pigeons in the world."

Aftermath

As a result of the investigation, several employees of the penitentiary resigned. Yet, the penal board cleared the Reverend William A. Huey, superintendent of the Girls (White) Industrial School, of the charges that he made "improper advances" toward one of the inmates and allowed Huey to resign. A minority report, nevertheless, thought Huey was guilty. The minority committee members recommended that men be excluded from positions of authority at the Women's Penitentiary and the Girls Industrial School.

Chapter 11

War on Vice

Part II/World War II

When the Japanese air force bombed the United States naval installation at Pearl Harbor, the United States once again found itself at war around the world. The Sunday morning attack on Pearl Harbor on December 7, 1941, not only ended the United States' isolation but also pushed the country into an unprecedented push toward military preparedness.

Part of that preparation centered on Columbia and the army facility known as Fort Jackson. Fort Jackson (formerly Camp Jackson) was a major processing and training facility for the United States Army. Recruits and draftees arrived in Columbia for basic training before assignments stateside or overseas.

In 1940, according to Janet Hudson in her article, "The Federal Government's Battle Against Venereal Disease During World War II: Implementation in South Carolina" published in the *Proceedings* of the South Carolina Historical Association in 1994, venereal disease, especially syphilis, was a major health threat. Untreated cases led to insanity, blindness and death. From 1936 forward, the United States surgeon general made eradicating venereal disease a major focus. With the approach of war, this campaign kicked into high gear. War always increased the rate of venereal disease, especially among military personnel. So with the outbreak of World War II, several health agencies worked with the armed services to combat the threat.

Part of the plan included controlling or even eliminating prostitution. Legislative action followed, and in 1941, Congress passed the May Act.

Fort Jackson enlistees at train station, by Curtiss B. Munn, 1940–41. *Courtesy of South Caroliniana Library, University of South Carolina (Photographs 12941-3).*

Under this legislation, prostitution near a military facility was a federal crime. The rationale for attacking prostitution was the argument that prostitution was the source of the majority of military venereal infections.

For South Carolina, the venereal disease situation was particularly distressing. During World War II, the draft act eliminated men with venereal disease from military service. For South Carolina draftees, the rate of rejection for venereal disease was three times the national average, giving South Carolina the second-highest rejection rate in the nation.

With South Carolina in such an unenviable position, national focus shifted to South Carolina military installations such as Fort Jackson and the Charleston Navy Yard. Military officials complained that local efforts, particularly around Fort Jackson, were ineffectual. While federal agents wanted prostitution eliminated, as Hudson noted, traditionally, South Carolina preferred to segregate brothels, rather than close them. Not only was South Carolina one of the states that did not legally ban prostitution but contracting with a prostitute was also legal in the state.

Fort Jackson enlistees in uniform with guns, by Curtiss B. Munn, 1940–41. *Courtesy of South Caroliniana Library, University of South Carolina (Photographs 12941-12).*

In March 1941, South Carolina had a new governor. Upon the death of Joseph E. Harley, Richard Manning Jefferies (1888–1964), president *pro tempore* of the South Carolina Senate, was sworn in as governor. During Jefferies's eleven months as governor, he worked to earn governmental military contracts. He took office at the time federal officials were pushing South Carolina to address the prostitution issue. As a result, in 1942, Jefferies sent a special message to the South Carolina House of Representatives stressing the need for a new law against prostitution. With federal pressure increasing, on March 14, 1942, the South Carolina legislature passed its first anti-prostitution law.

With the increased military presence in Columbia, brothels flourished as well, but Columbia mayor Frank Owens created a Committee on Social Hygiene to address the problem. The committee proposed a crackdown on houses of prostitution and more recreational activities for the soldiers. As a result, raids in Columbia's red-light district increased. Yet the city's efforts netted feeble results, and federal authorities increased their pressure on city authorities.

Fort Jackson tents, by Curtiss B. Munn, 1940–41. *Courtesy of South Caroliniana Library, University of South Carolina (Photographs 12941-10).*

With the development of penicillin, by 1944, there were effective treatment options for venereal disease. The focus then turned to developing treatment facilities—first for military personnel and then for prostitutes. While Jefferies supported such facilities, he insisted on two prostitution treatment sites—one for white women and one for black women. In time, his position prevailed, and South Carolina had two temporary facilities: Pontiac for white women and Goldville for black women. Generally, local police referred clients to these treatment sites. Most of the patients were "young women, fifteen to twenty-five years old, who had been arrested for prostitution." Once committed, the women had to complete their cure before they were released.

World War II ended in 1945, but neither problem disappeared. By the end of the war, military men were still contracting venereal disease, but prostitutes were no longer the main source. A sexual revolution was coming, and promiscuity was on the rise.

"What's Past Is Prologue"

In Columbia, ghost tours are popular pastimes. Many tour Elmwood and other local cemeteries, and others tout the ghosts of Columbia's historic houses, such as the Hampton Preston House or the Robert Mills House. But in Columbia, the ghosts of past vice and villainy also haunt the present. Public officials are still accused of improprieties, kidnapping and murder strike fear, gambling holds its allure and prostitution is still news.

For long-time Columbians, the cases of Dail Dinwiddie, who disappeared in 1992, and Dawn Smith echo the senseless horror of the Hubbard Harris case. Twenty years later, the Dinwiddie case remains an unsolved nightmare, while Larry Eugene Bell who kidnapped and killed Dawn Smith was arrested and executed. Evil may be discovered but not understood.

Prostitution is a recurring issue. For example, in September 1995, Sheriff Alan Sloan charged a Richland Northeast resident of operating a prostitution ring that included "prominent" Columbians. The woman in question advertised in the Yellow Pages as an escort service. Identified clients ranged from blue collar to professional, from mobile home dwellers to Wildewood residents. The operator was known as "Vannessa." The sheriff also arrested several other women and a man on charges of prostitution and operating a house of prostitution. These women apparently collected $130–$200 per hour. According to Lieutenant Andy Jones, the "going rate for street prostitutes is $25 to $50 per sexual favor."

More common are charges of solicitation. In 1989, Richland County Sheriff Alan Sloan charged thirteen men with soliciting prostitutes in the

Aerial view from State House grounds looking northeast—U.S. Post Office and Hotel Columbia, by Curtiss B. Munn, c. 1951. *Courtesy of South Caroliniana Library, University of South Carolina (Photographs 12941-19).*

2800 block of Two Notch Road. The sheriff contended that the arrests proved that the area of Two Notch was the center of the county's streetwalkers.

On December 11, 2012, the front-page headline of the *State* reported that "Most Want Tougher S.C. Ethics Laws." Why this push for ethics reform in 2012? The *State* cited state ethics investigations of former governor Mark Sanford, Lieutenant Governor Ken Ard and current governor Nikki Haley. As reported in the *State* on December 30, 2012, "The S.C. House Ethics Committee twice heard allegations that Gov. Nikki Haley used her position, as a state representative, to financially benefit herself or her employer (Lexington Medical Center)." Haley was cleared of ethics charges, but Sanford was not as fortunate. Thanks in part to the investigative reporting of Jim Davenport, Sanford was charged with using the state airplane to fly him to vacations and other personal appointments as well as failure to declare flights on private airplanes. Although he denied wrongdoing, in the end, Sanford pleaded no contest to thirty-seven ethics violations and paid a

Statehouse from Sumter Street. *Photograph by Jacob H. Helsley.*

$74,000 fine, plus $36,498 to cover the cost of the investigation. On the other hand, Ard, a Florence Republican, acknowledged his guilt and resigned.

In January 2013, gambling was in the news. According to the *State*, an Irmo-area double-murder investigation led authorities to a local sports betting operation. The accused murderer operated a sports booking enterprise that employed one of the victims. In the course of the investigation, sheriff's department investigators uncovered a large sports betting operation in the Columbia area. Those arrested and sentenced were involved in different aspects of the operation—financing, internet access and bet processing.

Vice and villainy are clearly still alive and well in Columbia. Traveling in the past makes familiar the present. As the Marquis de Sade said, "In order to know virtue, we must acquaint ourselves with vice."

Inhabitants of Richland County Jail, 1880

This snapshot illustrates the men incarcerated in the county jail. Criminals convicted of more serious crimes served their time at the state penitentiary.

NAME	HOME	CRIME
Hannibal Branham	Richland County	burglary and grand larceny
March Harris	Richland County	burglary and grand larceny
Washington Hart	City of Columbia	burglary
June Cornish	Richland County	burglary
Baxter Campbell	Town of York	grand larceny
James Heyward	City of Columbia	pickpocket
Samuel Green	City of Columbia	murder
Joseph Stevens	Edgefield County	murder

Select Bibliography

Edgar, Walter B., and Deborah K. Woolley. *Columbia: Portrait of a City*. Norfolk, VA: Donning Company, 1986.

Helsley, Alexia Jones. *Lost Columbia: Bygone Images of South Carolina's Capital City*. Charleston, SC: The History Press, 2009.

Hennig, Helen Kohn. *Columbia, Capital City of South Carolina 1783–1936, with supplement by Charles Lee, 1936–66*. Columbia, SC: State Record Company, 1966.

Hollis, Daniel Walker. *University of South Carolina, Volume I: South Carolina College; Volume II: College to University*. Columbia: University of South Carolina Press, 1951, 1956.

Lucas, Marion B. *Sherman and the Burning of Columbia*. Columbia: University of South Carolina Press, 2008.

Maxey, Russell. *Historic Columbia: Yesterday and Today in Photographs*. Columbia, SC: R.L. Bryan Company, 1980.

Montgomery, John A. *Columbia, South Carolina: History of a City*. Woodland Hills, CA: Windsor Publications, Inc., 1979.

Moore, John Hammond. *Columbia & Richland County: A South Carolina Community 1740–1990.* Columbia: University of South Carolina Press, 1993.

Scott, Edwin J. *Random Recollections of a Long Life: 1806 to 1876.* Columbia, SC: C.A. Calvo Jr., Printer, 1884.

Selby, Julian A. *Memorabilia and Anecdotal Reminiscences of Columbia, SC.* Columbia, SC: R.L. Bryan, 1905.

South Caroliniana Library and Institute for Southern Studies, eds. *A Columbia Reader.* Columbia, SC: R.L. Bryan, circa 1986.

Index

About the Author

Alexia Jones Helsley is passionate about South Carolina's history. An archivist and historian, Helsley currently teaches history at the University of South Carolina–Aiken and serves as chair of the Old Exchange Commission. Among her titles published by The History Press are *Lost Columbia: Bygone Images from South Carolina's Capital*; *Beaufort, South Carolina: A History*; *A Guide to Historic Beaufort, South Carolina*; *Wicked Beaufort* and *A History of North Carolina Wine*. Recipient of the Governor's Archives Award, Helsley is married with two children and lives in Columbia.